START UP Thailand
The Entrepreneurs' Journey

Philip C Zerrillo

Singapore Management University, Singapore

Havovi Joshi

Singapore Management University, Singapore

Pannapachr Itthiopassagul

Thammasat University, Thailand

World Scientific

NEW JERSEY · LONDON · SINGAPORE · BEIJING · SHANGHAI · HONG KONG · TAIPEI · CHENNAI · TOKYO

Published by

World Scientific Publishing Co. Pte. Ltd.
5 Toh Tuck Link, Singapore 596224
USA office: 27 Warren Street, Suite 401-402, Hackensack, NJ 07601
UK office: 57 Shelton Street, Covent Garden, London WC2H 9HE

British Library Cataloguing-in-Publication Data
A catalogue record for this book is available from the British Library.

START-UP THAILAND
The Entrepreneurs' Journey

ISBN 978-981-121-618-3 (hardcover)
ISBN 978-981-121-619-0 (ebook for institutions)
ISBN 978-981-121-620-6 (ebook for individuals)

For any available supplementary material, please visit
https://www.worldscientific.com/worldscibooks/10.1142/11710#t=suppl

Desk Editor: Sandhya Venkatesh

Typeset by Stallion Press
Email: enquiries@stallionpress.com

CONTENTS

PREFACE

This book is intended to capture the vision, the spirit, the passion and the determination of a unique set of companies in Thailand. We, the authors, hope that the stories, or rather entrepreneurial journeys, presented herein will provide inspiration to those seeking to explore the entrepreneurial life. They chronicle the people who have stepped up and changed their industry, even its very focus, and they reveal some fascinating backstories as well as the strong will to succeed despite significant failures.

Few of the firms in this book experienced a straight-line path to success. Many of them began a journey towards their intended goal, only to find a better path to a better place. At times, there was no path in the initial venture, as you will see with several of the tech firms, and new ventures were begun. In other cases, the core business needed to be substantially changed and rethought in the face of changing environments and evolving technologies or completely jettisoned. But one thing in common that their leadership teams shared was perseverance and the passion to move forward, and 'get things done'.

Whether it began as a family business, or a group of friends that got together with the idea of doing something new, the Thai entrepreneurs featured in this book display the "Jai Dee" (good heart) that can only be found in Thailand. With a love for their King, their country, their family and their friends, these rising business leaders told us their stories and the journeys of their heart.

Khup Khun Mak Krup, thank you very much.

ACKNOWLEDGMENTS

This book would not have been possible without the support of several of people. We offer our sincere thanks and gratitude to the following organisations and people.

At the outset, we appreciate the support of the senior management at Singapore Management University. We would also like to extend our special thanks to our colleagues at the Centre for Management Practice. In particular, we wish to acknowledge Grace Segran. Thank you also to Irene Soh, Lim Wee Kiat, Adina Wong, Lipika Bhattacharya, Cheah Sin Mei, CW Chan, Sarita Mathur, Sheetal Bharadwaj, Alvin Lee, Sheila Wan, Tan Suhwen and Thomas Lim.

We also offer our appreciation to Thammasat University, especially Piyapa Narararak (Qing) and Sirinadda Kaweewattana (Peace) at the Masters in Marketing program, who made it possible for us to interview a number of the entrepreneurs showcased in this book.

And last, but most important, to each of those sterling entrepreneurs featured herein, thank you for taking the time to share your story with us.

Dr. Philip Zerrillo
Dr. Havovi Joshi
Ms. Pannapachr Itthiopassagul

Chapter 1

AN INTRODUCTION TO THAI ENTREPRENEURSHIP

A founding member of ASEAN, Thailand is the second largest economy in Southeast Asia (SEA). At the centre of the Greater Mekong Sub-region, an area that is home to more than half of ASEAN's 647 million inhabitants, Thailand is strategically well-located, sharing borders with Myanmar, Cambodia, Laos, and Malaysia. With a developed road system and six international airports, the country is well connected to its regional and international neighbours. Controlling the only land route between Greater Asia and Myanmar, Malaysia, and Singapore, it is ideally positioned to be a regional logistics hub.

Thailand was a country that invested heavily and early in developing its road ways, leading to agricultural and manufacturing efficiencies. Its connectivity has been exceptional by ASEAN standards. Unlike its regional neighbours — Indonesia and the Philippines that face theconnectivity challenges posed by thousands of distant islands, and Vietnam, Cambodia, Laos, and Myanmar that have under-invested in rails, roads, and ports by multiple trillions of dollars — Thailand has garnered efficiencies for businesses and the opportunity for entrepreneurs to serve a large single domestic market of about 68 million people and to reach international markets as well.

From 1985–1997, Thailand was ASEAN's fastest growing economy and one of the leading members of what were popularly termed the 'Tiger Economies' of SEA. Its central location and its logistical prowess put it near the top of any regional list for international investors. The country is ranked at or near the top in industries such as tourism, medical tourism, automotive manufacturing and supply, agriculture, processed food exports, and the like.

With an estimated internet penetration rate in 2018 of about 60%,[1] Thailand is rapidly moving into the digital economy as you will see from several of the companies that are profiled. With strong enthusiasm from the Thai government for digital and mobile technologies, Thailand shows some of the region's strongest engagement in social media. A February 6, 2018 Bangkok Post headline reads: "Thailand tops internet usage charts" with 9.38 hours per day usage rate.[2] Capitalising on these trends, the Thai authorities are increasing their support to start-ups, with the ultimate goal of modernising the economy through their vision "Thailand 4.0".[3] This appetite for the digital experience is creating opportunities and disruptions that we see in many of the businesses profiled.

The industry and service sectors produce about 90% of GDP, with agriculture contributing to the remaining 10%.[4] The number of employed persons in agriculture first began to fall in 1989, and its percentage share of total employment was overtaken by the non-agricultural sector in the late 1990s. Today an estimated one-third of Thailand's population is involved in the agriculture sector — down from 70% in 1980.[5] This transition has led to a growth in major cities and spurred new opportunities. With higher disposable incomes and greater sophistication, Thai consumers have continued to increase their expectations for products and services. Be it new brands, the provision of convenience or value-added services,

Thailand is witnessing the emergence of the modern society, side by side with the traditional. While wet markets and mom-and-pop stores continue to garner the lion's share of the market, modern trade has been growing at a startling rate, projected to grow by over 7% in 2019, from 1.77 trillion baht in 2018.[6] Few retail firms have been able to stand pat.

When one studies the business sectors of Thailand, it is quickly noticed that the country does not lack in entrepreneurial spirit. In fact, Thailand perennially ranks among the most entrepreneurial nations in the world. The Global Entrepreneurship Monitor survey for 2016–17 reported that Thailand's established-business ownership rate of 27.5 percent is the second highest among 65 countries polled. The report also stated that Thais are generally undeterred by the fear of business failures, and ranked the country as third highest in that category among all nations in the survey.[7] This is interesting given that the Thai education system largely discourages risk-taking behaviour — discussion and debate rarely play a part in their learning process.[8]

Entrepreneurs are typically well-respected and assigned a high status in Thai society. This holds true for the women as well; in fact, the entrepreneurship rate among females actually exceeds that of males in both nascent and on-going businesses.[9]

As mentioned, Thailand was home to one of the most rapid growing economies in the world during the last two decades of the 20th century. However, Thailand has also witnessed periods of great uncertainty and calamity. With three coups in the past thirty years, the Asian Financial Crisis of 1997 (also termed the Tom Yum Kung crisis), the Global Financial Crisis of 2008, an outbreak of SARS and bird flu, and the great tsunami which wreaked havoc on Thailand's second largest area of commerce (Phuket) — the entrepreneurs of Thailand have had to learn how to be resilient. The positive spirit and hope for a better tomorrow, despite the problems of the day, was evident each time we spoke with a business owner. In the pages and stories that follow, we hope you will be able to see why Thailand is home to many determined and clever entrepreneurs.

Endnotes

1. Statista, Internet user penetration in Thailand from 2017 to 2023, https://www.statista.com/statistics/975067/internet-penetration-rate-in-thailand/Statista2018.
2. Suchit Leesa-Nguansuk, "Thailand tops internet usage charts", Bangkok Post, 6 February 2018.
3. ASEAN Up, https://aseanup.com/business-thailand/.
4. CIA World Factbook, "Thailand", July 2018.
5. Nipon Poapongsakorn, "The decline and recovery of Thai agriculture: causes, responses, prospects and challenges", http://www.fao.org/3/ag089e/AG089E04.htm, 2006.
6. Phusadee Arunmas, "Modern trade set to see surge", Bangkok Post, May 2019.
7. The Nation Thailand, "Thailand has what is needed for entrepreneurs", 31 March 2017, https://www.nationthailand.com/Corporate/30310947.
8. Krating Poonpol, "Bringing Silicon Valley to Thailand", Singapore Management University, Asian Management Insights. 3(1), 84–88, 2016.
9. Minniti, Allen, & Langowitz, "The Global Entrepreneurship Monitor study of entrepreneurs identified the emerging patterns of participation of women", 2005.

SECTION 1: Entrepreneurship: A Family Business

Family businesses are nothing new to this part of the world. Japan's Takenaka Corporation, for example, has been around since 1610, when a shrine and temple carpenter set up shop in Nagoya; the family has been able to overcome business, political, and family threats for more than four centuries. Several empirical studies have reported that individuals who come from families with an entrepreneurial member are more likely to become entrepreneurs themselves. It is hence a virtuous circle that gets established, and research shows this holds true for Thailand.[1]

The successful businesses mentioned below are a mixture of established firms, brought to life by younger family members who studied in Thailand or overseas, and introduced their new knowledge into the family's business models. As the interviews reveal — teams, talent, education, and continuing education is the key.

For instance, the rise of Jubilee Enterprise PCL, a ninety-year old jewellery firm, where the father and daughter's far-sighted manoeuvres transformed a venerable single-store Bangkok jewellery institution into a prosperous twenty-first century public-listed company with 125 retail outlets. Together, the pair infused Jubilee, with the same passion and entrepreneurial spirit that characterises the world's leading diamond and *haute joaillerie* houses — reflecting Bangkok's status as one of the world's great gemstone capitals.

In another peek into Thailand's family hives, it is true to say that the challenges of the transition to a second generation are neither necessarily straightforward nor an easy path to navigate. Take growth, for example, and the need to do different things differently and still continue to blaze trails, a frequent demand made by a firm's younger generation. A common challenge lies in balancing the diverse interests of family members while at the same time having to share a common goal. Opinions must be counted and strategies should be adjusted accordingly. Patcharapan Vanadurongwan, the chief operating officer of Vichaivej International Hospital Group, brought these interests together and grew the small clinic started by her parents thirty years ago into a publicly listed international hospital group. Critical to the Group's success were some adroit changes in ownership and succession planning, which were needed to secure the futures of her generation and the generations to follow.

Succession planning is now considered important for attracting investment. In mid-August 2014, the Economist Intelligence Unit conducted a research study of 250 majority family-owned businesses from Indonesia, Malaysia, the Philippines, Singapore, and Thailand, and noted that sixty-seven percent of these family businesses had implemented such succession plans, while seventy-four percent of executives said they are integral for growth and that consumers believe the presence of succession planning instils trustworthiness.[2]

In the case of Sappe, another family-run enterprise that is now publicly listed on the Stock Exchange of Thailand — attendance at a local food science conference a decade ago provided a springboard for the Thai beverage company to secure a global presence. Its transition from a small-scale traditional snack manufacturer and vendor reflects a constant strive for innovation and it has since entered the growing health and beauty beverage sector. Interestingly, Chief Operating Officer, Arnupap Ruckariyapong, said he found public listings to be important to the sustainability and success of future generations.

Endnotes

1. Kilenthong, W. & Rueanthip, K., "Entrepreneurship and family businesses in Thailand", Asian-Pacific Economic Literature, 2018.
2. The Economist Intelligence Unit, "Building legacies: Family business succession in South-east Asia", 2014.

Chapter 2

JUBILEE: PASSION AND THE ENTREPRENEURIAL SPIRIT

The decision to incorporate the understated elegance of black into a signature element of its key outlets subtly underscores the far-sighted manoeuvres that transformed a ninety-year-old Bangkok jewellery institution into a prosperous twenty-first century public-listed company with 125 retail outlets. The rise of Jubilee Enterprise PCL echoes the very same passions and entrepreneurial spirit that characterise the world's leading jewellery houses. It's a remarkable story.

When it comes to gold and diamonds, Asian cities are legendary. Every city has them: some are no more than outdoor stalls located up narrow alleyways, others lurk in the ground floors of shop houses, while the older well-known ones sprawl across two or three lots, sometimes extending a precarious storey or two upwards. Nowadays, several have made the journey to the High Street. Jubilee Diamonds, for example, began as a family business in Bangkok's old Chinatown almost ninety years ago.

Four generations later, it is still in the diamond business, but has now spread far and wide across Thailand, says Unyarat Pornprakit, the youthful Chief Executive Officer of Jubilee Enterprise PCL — a diamond jewellery retailer listed on the Stock Exchange of Thailand, of which glamorous newcomer — Jubilee of Siam — is part. A former auditor at PricewaterhouseCoopers Thailand, Unyarat joined the family firm as a cost officer. At that time, she was considering going abroad to complete her master's degree, but discovered an unexpected passion for the industry — 'it's in her DNA' as her father puts it — and she decided to combine work and study at Bangkok's Thammasat University, Masters in Marketing program.

Unyarat's approach to marketing and product innovation builds on the revolutionary steps in diamond jewellery retailing her father had introduced more than twenty years ago. In those days, with department stores opening in the suburbs of Bangkok, he observed presciently that customers would start shopping more and more at these outlets, rather than buying from the traditional diamond stores at the street side shops of the big cities.

In his view, the time was right for 'a diamond shop in a department store format' — that is smaller, more geographically dispersed outlets at large stores that would enhance accessibility for the consumer and also require lower capital to operate than a traditional stand-alone jewellery store. This was a concept that radically changed the sales and distribution of diamond jewellery in Thailand. A large part of this was to do with trust. Four generations ago, traditional outlets attracted a neighbourhood clientele. The buyer and seller knew one another. People bought directly from the owner — or his family — rather than from sales staff. Relationships of trust were nurtured carefully. But that changed with the debut of the 'diamond counter' format in which sales staff took over the role of the owner.

Founding Jubilee Diamonds

"My father commenced Jubilee Diamonds in 1993 and went on to open ten diamond counters in ten different department stores (the first one was opened at the old Yao Han department store). By 1995, his original ten stores had shot up to fifty, which is when I joined. He's a fast mover", said Unyarat.

However, the reluctance on the customers' part to trust the sales staff saw the business run at a loss for the first two or three years but he persevered — acquiring 2,000 new clients in that period — compared with just about 100 from the old store that had been operating for nearly 90 years.

Revenue-wise too, the move was not without its problems. "When people buy from the owner, they buy higher value items", explained Unyarat, but when they bought from sales staff, they were more cautious and bought lower-priced items, as the trust relationship was yet to develop.

In just three years, he had created the forerunner of the modern Jubilee Enterprise, transforming and restructuring it with sales, marketing, and production departments.

Interestingly, for an Asian firm, it also emphasised competency over educational attainments.

Market Strategies

While it could be expected that there was a large marketing team that stood behind Jubilee to support its multiple locations — in fact the marketing team was not large at that time, but it was innovative, adjusting its marketing strategy in 1997 ahead of a significant shop counter expansion into major malls.

Unyarat mentions that her father believed that consumer confidence in the product was the key to market expansion. Some of the tactics he used were challenging, if not confronting, for its competitors, "We were the first to display diamond prices on the billboard outside the shop in Chinatown. Passers-by looked at the prices. Our competitors complained because we were advertising the price publicly, making it difficult for them to significantly mark-up their wares, or so they said". Today such promotional activities may be termed disruptive, but it also led to the question whether he was promoting diamonds as a commodity or as the Jubilee brand. "Jubilee Diamonds", she responds without hesitation.

A further innovation involved pitching on the basis of the 'standout price' for a one-carat diamond. In Thailand, this was quite a proposition as it involved educating consumers about the standout price, or 'Rapaport' as it is known. The weekly *Rapaport Report,* founded by Martin Rapaport in 1978, is the jewellery industry standard for the pricing of diamonds and is issued to jewellers and diamond merchants. Diamonds are priced based on the 4 Cs — carat, colour, clarity, and cut. This could ruffle quite a few feathers. Normally, says Unyarat, "Sellers do not want their customers to know about the Rapaport, because they want to sell at their individual preferred price. It's where their margins are".

In addition to relatively conventional promotions, albeit high-end, such as premium diamonds on television game shows, cross promotion with Mercedes to grab the big spenders, and loyalty programs, Unyarat's father also utilised a newsletter. This was a first for the Thai diamond industry. It meant that around seventy percent of people coming to the store had already viewed the product. "All the sales staff had to do was provide the remaining thirty percent of the service. Then close the sale".

In another unique marketing twist, her father revelled in the tactical use of colour — counters were changed to blue and silver, while staff wore different coloured uniforms on the days of the week: yellow on Monday, pink on Tuesday, green on Wednesday, and so forth. This provided customers with a consistent experience at the counter, part of engaging with them and building trust through consistency.

When Unyarat joined the company — putting price tags on the stock, no less — her father encouraged her to continue her studies and become a gemologist, which she did. Grading diamonds was the next logical step. "When I learned I could do it, I began to develop a passion about the business", she said, "and began to talk the 'diamond language'".

While her father's idea of building the brand was based on trust, Unyarat's focus was to take it to the next level by employing a more comprehensive marketing mix as a brand driver. In 2001, to grow the business further, Jubilee sought to wrest consumers from the traditional outlets, using cross promotion with Krungthai Leasing Co. Ltd. (a subsidiary of the Krung Thai Bank group), a retail consumer leasing company that offered the option to pay by instalments. Although partnering with a bank added credibility in the minds of consumers, it also emphasised the end of the trust relationship with the owner that had been a hallmark of the old traditional business model. While it seemed less personal, it was infinitely more scalable.

Even today, the company's outlet-expansion strategy still remains closely tied to its retail developer partners in major shopping complexes and department stores.

Franchising

While the growth in outlets was rapid, the required capital was not easy to come by as this novel concept began to take hold but was yet to be highly profitable. Franchising was an early inspiration and her father travelled to the provinces and sold franchises to the region's wealthy, a move that saw the company's outlets expand to 50, half of which were owned outright while the remainder were franchised. The franchising concept allowed the firm to gain unprecedented scale in the Thai market. Moreover, it pacified the department stores, which came to rely on Jubilee to anchor the diamond section of their jewellery departments. Additionally, the scale of operations began to attract first tier diamond suppliers to the Thai market as they could now gain a foothold without having to vet numerous small fragmented resellers.

Unyarat's father was quick to realise that anyone is capable of generating income for the business, not only the owner. He created a new job in Thailand, the 'Diamond Advisor', which enabled non-business owners to make money from selling diamonds. The fresh approach to management meant the business could now offer job opportunities, unheard of in the old style businesses, and a good income as a means of optimising the efficient use of talent in order to create competitiveness.

Listening to the details of the franchising strategy and process, one is reminded of H. Stern, the luxury jewellery brand. When Hans Stern arrived in Rio Janeiro in 1945, he travelled inland on horseback, getting to know the miners and the lodes of tourmalines, amethysts, topazes, and other semiprecious stones in the backwoods. He raised the Brazilian jewellery trade to international standards, later franchising one hundred and seventy H. Stern outlets in twenty-six countries.[1]

But while franchising helped to infuse capital and gain scale, there were risks involved. In each store and at every counter, the Jubilee name was present and franchisees needed to uphold the consistency and service experience that would build the brand. Unyarat added that there is a tendency to be 'nice' with the franchisees because they've put their money up — they're the smaller one in the relationship — but by the same token, they can also let service or quality fall and "suddenly you don't have a brand". They will also have their own opinion on how to run the business, their own style if you will. "If you are able to comply, you can ride with us, but if it's too much, it's also okay. We'll take it back", she says. Which is exactly what they did.

As a result, the franchising operations ceased during Unyarat's time, as her vision for the brand was far more refined than her father's and required the franchisees to invest in the brand — which they may not have been willing to do. In any event, the company's objectives too had changed and it was now endeavouring to introduce product and service standardisation across the country, which would have been difficult if the franchises were still afoot.

By 2017, Jubilee had one hundred and twenty-five stores nationwide, all of them owned outright. This appeared to be a rapid leap, where the size and extent of the inventory alone, for example, would have been enough to strangle the average jewellery outlet. In general though, jewellery is not a high turnover industry, which means mastering an efficient inventory management system is a key success factor, as the experience of firms such as the Zale Corporation[2] in the United States shows.

Certification for the Cautious Consumer

Buyers were understandably apprehensive in the absence of an established relationship with the seller and made lower value purchases. The shifting sands of the buyer-seller trust relationship now needed urgent attention if sales were to increase. Diamond prices were soaring hand in hand with a high level of standardisation in the global industry. Similarly, unscrupulous sellers often sought to keep consumers in the dark and would tell them anything just to make a sale, adds Unyarat.

The solution was a certificate attesting to the quality of the diamond that could then be given to the buyer and, in 2007, Jubilee added certification to its marketing arsenal.

The process of certification was introduced by Unyarat's father, and began with certification of one carat size and above diamonds from Hoge Raad voor Diamant (HRD), the leading authority in diamond certification in Europe, together with international certification from the Gemological Institute of America (GIA). Jubilee's counter at the Pan Pacific Hotel, Bangkok, was the only loose diamond focused shop in Thailand to sell HRD-certified diamonds.

Jubilee insists that its diamond suppliers are listed on the De Beers Global Sightholder Sales (DBGSS), and does not buy conflict or blood diamonds, a reference to diamonds mined in war zones and sold, unethically, to fund rebel groups. HRD is not otherwise to be found in Thailand, and has market acceptance only due to Jubilee.

The Gemological Institute of America (GIA), established in 1931, is the world's foremost authority on diamonds, coloured stones, and pearls. In the 1940s, GIA introduced the famous 4Cs: cut, which provides its sparkle and brilliance; clarity, or the absence of blemishes; colour, ranked from D-to-Z with the less colour the higher the value; and carat, with one carat equal to 0.2 grams. Together, the 4Cs comprise the International Diamond Grading System™, which still remains the worldwide standard for evaluating diamond quality.

Protecting consumer confidence remains of paramount importance to the long-term success of the industry, as noted recently by World Jewellery Confederation (CIBJO) president Gaetano Cavalieri in *The Diamond Terminology Guideline* (January 2018), which sought to standardise the terminology used in the industry. The same can be said for Jubilee.

Daring Decisions

A New Look

Before the launch of Jubilee of Siam in May 2015, Unyarat's own innovation had taken the company one-step further. Under her stewardship, Jubilee has moved from a counter-based sales point, to 'islands' — basically counters with a virtual space in which sofas are placed strategically within a freestanding area. The new ambience generates exclusivity, she says, and a new customer experience. "They feel more relaxed — and spend more".

She also made a major decision to change all the counters to black as the signature colour. While black is a premium colour, the change might have been problematic. "As Thai Chinese, we're mostly allergic to black. But my father is quite open-minded and after going back and forth about it for a while, we proceeded to renovate all the stores".

A daring decision it was, but black has been a coveted thematic in the couture end of the fashion market for generations; Chanel and Karl Lagerfeld being prime examples. The company did extensive market research to see if the customer would embrace the colour scheme, and found it was highly regarded. It was also a major investment. "We didn't just change the colour; we changed the total look of the brand, added inventory, and professionalised the sales staff. We are now doing more than just selling diamond jewellery; we have our own design team and create our own designs". The relocation to Sathorn — the upmarket financial and commerce district — was another sound move. The decisions paid off, and sales grew store-on-store by double-digits.

Product Innovation

Company growth and its insistence on international standards have seen Jubilee begin to surface on the radar of suppliers of the big houses like the Italian Luxury brand, Bulgari. "'Who is this guy in a small country buying so many diamonds?'" was the whisper in these circles. Suppliers also began to offer high-quality goods exclusively to Jubilee.

Now big enough, Jubilee was able to reach out directly to suppliers such as De Beers, which meant they could access super quality and rare classifications of diamonds in volume.

New raw materials, new manufacturing techniques, and technology that were once only available in the very developed global markets became available to Jubilee. Designs are innovative and the focus is on the quality of the diamond. Even Japan's ambassador for the 2025 Osaka World Expo, Hello Kitty, has made her way into the Jubilee collection (the only one in Thailand with the license for Hello Kitty for diamond jewellery), possibly reflecting a younger moneyed demographic.

Unyarat commented that when suppliers to brands like Bulgari and Tiffany see the quality of Jubilee's products, they are very impressed by the complexity and details in design that have been put together into a solid jewellery piece and always ask, "'Why aren't you selling this to the world?' 'Why keep this in Thailand?' And my answer is, 'Well, we need more people. We're trying.'"

A New Brand

This kind of cutting-edge product innovation was possible in Unyarat's time, as she had already positioned the brand successfully at the top-end. Once the brand successfully achieved a premium perception — that is when the expansion really started. There was an increasing interaction with more and more high-end people, and in December 2016, Jubilee Enterprise announced plans for two physical stores under two strategic brands, Jubilee Diamond, a brand owned by the company, and Forevermark, the diamond brand owned by De Beers Group for which Jubilee Enterprise is Thailand's exclusive authorised distributor and retailer (including e-commerce, although the focus of its outlet expansion in Thailand will be bricks and mortar stores). "The business plans for the two brands are different in their direction and each will contribute to the company in a different way", she said.[3]

Forevermark is new to Thailand. At present, only three of Jubilee's outlets carry Forevermark, the number one global diamond brand. Unyarat is hoping to have another five outlets by the end of the year.

Rebirth

Several years ago, McKinsey considered the future of the jewellery industry in 2020, now only a couple of years away. "A glittering prospect", they enthused, "buoyed by the possibility of enormous global sales and a growing consumer appetite for jewellery".[4]

Jubilee Diamonds listed on the Stock Exchange of Thailand (SET) in 2009, becoming Jubilee Enterprise PCL (JUBILE: TB), after which a huge brand transformation occurred. At that time, Unyarat said, people laughed at the idea of an IPO for a jewellery firm, reasoning that if you made everything public, and opened up the innermost workings of the company, you'd be finished. But this has been the way of many of the world's leading brands — Tiffany & Co and the Swatch Group (which acquired the legendary Harry Winston) are public companies, while in Southeast Asia, Malaysia's Poh Kong Holdings Berhad is listed on the Bursa Malaysia (KLSE), and Lee Hwa (Aspial Corporation) on the Singapore Stock Exchange (SGX).

However, it was the reason for the IPO that surprised everyone. While sales really started booming post-IPO, it wasn't for that purpose or ego on her father's part, she said. "He wanted to do business in the proper way, and be able to turn around and say [proudly] 'OK, we are taxpayers'".

The other reason was probably just as prescient as the decision twenty years earlier to open a store within a store, as she explains: "The diamond jewellery business is a very closed one in Thailand, only a few people understand it, and there is only a small group of customers. He reasoned that if we did an IPO, it would open up and expand the market as well as bring greater market opportunities".

Its public listing reflects a long journey from a small store in Chinatown ninety years ago to Jubilee Enterprise PCL, and the refinements made to its marketing strategy over the years: "To lead the retail diamond jewellery business in Thailand through the development of diamond sales in a transparent manner, disclosing the correct information to the customer, and adjusting customer attitudes to meet with international practice".

The fresh capital went on to fund corporate expansion, Information Technology (IT), and inventory; around one hundred and fifteen outlets were opened after the IPO.

The IPO took two years to prepare and it was an arduous process. "There were no benchmarks", she adds "and the regulators had no idea about the diamond business". Filing took nine months with "every single page bouncing back and forth". She even had to go to the regulator herself. Here, the experience from her master's program proved invaluable, especially participation in the Global Moot Corp®, a venture competition for business schools around the world held in Austin, Texas.[5] "I actually thought it was tougher to present at the global competition than back here in Bangkok".

The public listing totally changed the organisation, strategically and practically, and it meant addressing a host of verifiable parameters. One of the first things Unyarat did was to increase sales goals, relocate certain stores, and expand the space in others in order to create more sales. Today Jubilee's shares are at ten times the IPO value, and it continues to be the only retail diamond jewel brand listed on the SET.

The company now employs hundreds of people. When asked about her 'operating philosophy', she responds by saying that it is a combination of company performance and the welfare or happiness of the employees: "The people are the most important. If they're happy, I'm happy".

Endnotes

1. The New York Times, "Hans Stern Dies at 85; Built Global Jewelry Empire", 29 October 2007, http://www.nytimes.com/2007/10/29/world/americas/29stern.html.
2. Acquired by Signet in 2014, Zale was one of the largest specialty jewellery retailers in the world in its day. Probably best known for its marketing strategy, "a penny down and a dollar a week," it introduced the concept of mass marketing and made jewellery affordable.
3. Kwanchai Rungfapaisarn, "Jubilee Enterprise plans stores for two diamond brands", *The Nation*, 12 December 2016, http://www.nation multimedia.com/detail/Corporate/30301977.
4. Linda Dauriz, Nathalie Remy, and Thomas Tochtermann, "A multifaceted future: The jewelry industry in 2020", McKinsey.com, Febuary 2014, https://www.mckinsey.com/industries/retail/our-insights/a-multifaceted-future-the-jewelry-industry-in-2020.
5. The competition is considered the most prestigious of its kind. The Thammasat MIM program has been participating since 1997 and is the only school from Asia to have won it twice, once in 1995 and once in 2005.

Chapter 3

VICHAIVEJ INTERNATIONAL HOSPITAL GROUP: THE CHALLENGES OF BEGINNING THE SECOND GENERATION

With first generation companies, their struggles and successes always make for fascinating reading. The transition to a second generation is not necessarily straightforward. And nor is it an easy path. Take growth, for example, the need to do different things differently and still continue to blaze trails. Patcharapan Vanadurongwan, the chief operating officer of Vichaivej International Hospital Group, explains how the small clinic started by her parents thirty years ago expanded successfully to a publicly-listed international hospital group, elaborating on the changes in ownership and succession planning that were needed to secure the futures of her generation and the generations that will follow.

Medical tourism, or tourist travel for the purpose of receiving medical treatment or improving health or fitness, is a growing industry in Thailand brought on by the spiralling cost of healthcare in many countries around the world, the ease of travel, and an increasingly mobile workforce. Most governments cannot afford to build hospitals, which provides the private sector with the opportunity to step up and meet the demand for healthcare in regions where there's undercoverage. In the case of Thailand, the low cost of medical treatment and the acknowledged high quality of treatment provided by private medical centres are driving forces in the industry, which has bloomed since the early-2000s. There are now more than one thousand hospitals in the country, of which more than four hundred and seventy are private facilities. Thai doctors are attracted to the international hospitals as they can typically earn much more there than in the public hospitals.

Investors too are seeking to enter the lucrative field. And; why not? With ageing populations that are living longer and the ability to influence the length of the customers demand cycle through excellent treatment, health care is a unique opportunity.

Investment is not cheap — medical equipment and technologies are very expensive and prone to disruptive changes and processes. There is also the need to address the new reality of patient rights, engagement, and advocacy, which differs from the old hospital management system models of over thirty years ago. In Thailand, the size of the investment required has seen the quest for funding land in the capital markets. Twenty hospitals are now listed on the Stock Exchange of Thailand (SET), a sector dominated by Bangkok Dusit Medical Services, Thailand's largest private healthcare group founded by Thai billionaire Prasert Prasarttong-Osoth, and Bumrungrad International Hospital, a private multiple-specialty medical centre founded in 1980.

Three basic investment models are used by would-be hospital investors. The first sells know how, or consulting services, with hefty management fees charged for a set period of time, enabling the hospitals to remain profitable as well as boost their overall margins and returns to shareholders with limited physical investment. The second focuses on merger and acquisition, involving the acquisition of distressed hospitals or hospitals that are undervalued because they lack the professional management needed. The third is capital intensive and relies on owning and operating a hospital.

In the case of the public-listed Vichaivej International Hospital Group, which began as a family enterprise thirty years ago and is now seeking international expansion side by side with meeting the needs of a burgeoning domestic market, a fourth strategy is used: following and responding to government policy. In addition to meeting the need of the government's universal health coverage plans, the Group also seeks opportunities available under Thailand's relatively new economic policies.

Complicating the investment equation is the fact that hospitals are generally location-based businesses, like retailers, while, like hotels, hospitals will also need to measure occupancy rates, typically around eighty percent. If the rates are increased, further investment is needed, which in turn puts a lot of strain on an organisation's performance.

Patcharapan Vanadurongwan, better known as Pyn, is the daughter of the founders of the Vichaivej International Hospital Group. Her father, Vichai Vanadurongwan, a well-known orthopaedist — a physician who corrects congenital or functional abnormalities of the bones with surgery, casting, and bracing, as well as treats injuries to the bones — established the business with his wife, a pathologist. Impeccably credentialed, he has been able to draw on a wide network developed from his time in academia, Asia-wide sports interests, and sports medicine, as well as in advisory positions to several government ministries. He is considered the founder of sports medicine in Thailand.

"Doctors can always be happy just practicing medicine. But my parents were passionate about starting a business", Pyn said. "Nothing was impossible for the two of them". Thirty years ago, when her father established the business, orthopaedic clinics, such as the one at Siriraj Medical School,[1] where he was working, were so crowded that patients even placed their shoes on the floor to mark a place in the lengthy queues. Doctors, too, she added, had exhausting practice schedules, with hospitals operating on a virtual twenty-four hour basis. "He was at the hospital from eight to five, his main operating hours, and was then available from five to eight to attend to patients who needed to see a doctor after hours".

He questioned how patients could be better served and went on to open the Samyaekfaichai Poly Clinic, the nucleus of what would later become the Vichaivej International Hospital Group. As soon as his patients knew he had his own clinic, they came to him.

"My father is not quite like a doctor, he's more of a visionary and businessman, who also happens to be an orthopaedist. My mother, on the other hand, is more of a follower, helping the family dream to come true, and is happy to support him no matter what. She managed the business, while my father took care of the patients".

Pyn was born after the first hospital branch was established, which, she said, meant she had practically grown up with the hospital.

The "Generals"

When the clinic had been operating for around a year or two, Vichai decided to turn the clinic into a hospital. This meant obtaining a hospital license and then registering the company as a hospital. To do this, he had to invest in inpatient beds. It was a swift process, she said. The Samyaekfaichai Poly Clinic now became the Srivichai Hospital, a name that reflected her father's name. "'Vichai' is derived from my father's name while 'sri' means 'good' in Thai". It was also the name of an ancient civilisation located in southern Thailand, which he admired. "Our hospital too is located in the southern part of Bangkok".

Her parents rented the premises for the hospital and began the staffing process. This proved to be a challenge. Five people were recruited; a small team that her father and mother affectionately dubbed the "generals". Not all of the five had medical skills. "My parents were at the helm of the business, like a king and queen, supported by a team of trusted and able 'generals'".

Despite the title, the generals had to do everything from scrubbing floors to paperwork to dealing with clients and suppliers. As time went by, her parents became the sole owners of a second, third, and fourth hospital and rewarded the generals for their loyalty by including them in the owner's team. When they opened the second and third hospitals, the next generation of five generals was recruited. They in turn were managed by one of the generals from the original management team.

The 'king', 'queen', and 'generals' were also quite entrepreneurial, she said, and in the case of Pyn, more like family. With the family home situated on top of the building, the hospital was an early playground, where she knew everyone from the generals to employees. Literally growing up in the hospital, the staff were the people she saw and talked to every day.

Successive hospital acquisitions still reflect Srivichai's focus on providing quality services for patients, specialised medical treatment combined with preventive measures, and an integrated approach to holistic medicine, supported by advanced technology and medical equipment. "It is a patient-focused philosophy", she said. Her father had started the original clinic as a means to provide better service and care to the patients who waited for long hours just for a consultation at the government-run hospitals. "He knew there had to be a better way to deliver care, and that principle continues to drive the company today", she added.

In the last few years, the Group and its subsidiaries have signed MoUs with universities and colleges for academic and practical training, as well as sports, insurance, standard, and quality certifications.

Two key tenets that have guided the firm's decisions have been geographic expansion (rather than a rapid growth in the breath of medical services), both locally and internationally; as well as offering services within Thailand to accommodate foreign clients or patients.

Economic Policies and Investment Opportunities

One of the strategies underpinning the success of the Group was to leverage the potential of the government's economic policies. The first of these dates back to the mid to the late 1990s when the government sought to reduce congestion in Bangkok by persuading manufacturers to relocate outside the cities, a move it thought would be followed by young people in search of work in the factories. In some cases, tax incentives were introduced to persuade businesses to move to these outlying districts.

For his part, her father had already noted that central Bangkok had many hospitals and healthcare services. To serve the community better, he headed to southern Bangkok on the outskirts of the city where, in 1993, he established the polyclinic that became the basis for his first fully-fledged and registered hospital.

Almost twenty years later, in 2014, the Thai government adopted the Special Economy Zone (SEZ) model into its policy system. In total, ten SEZs were to be introduced along the borders across the country: Tak and Kanchanaburi, which border Myanmar, Chiang Rai on the Thailand-Lao-Myanmar border; Mukdaharn, Nong Khai, and Nakhon Phanom on the Thailand-Laos border; Trat and Sa Kaew on the Thailand-Cambodia border; and Songkhla and Narathiwas in the southern part of Thailand that borders Malaysia.[2] This was also taking place at the time of the regional connectivity proposed under the ASEAN Economic Community (AEC), which was aimed at connecting all Southeast Asian countries using one road. These policies were intended to shift many of the nations' demographic trends, and infrastructure spending was following alongside.

With three hospitals in his portfolio, her father viewed the upcoming SEZ and AEC policies as the basis for further investment, spurred by an injection of fresh capital from the Group's public listing in 2012.

As the Group moved into the zones[3] and the provinces that had been set aside, it worked with manufacturers that were also transitioning to the same regions. "Their employees need access to healthcare and their employers don't want to have to take multiple plans and multiple payers", she said. And, as in many other countries, rural healthcare remains a huge problem, but one that can bring investment opportunities.

There are now four hospitals in the Vichaivej International Hospital Group. All are general hospitals, although their base remains orthopaedics, with athletes, accidents, work-related injuries, and orthopaedic care forming major revenue streams.

Business Focus

The Group focuses on middle to high-income clients and patients. "We also have to take care of the middle income patients as well", said Pyn. Although wealthy Thais might still go abroad to Singapore or Korea for medical services, the Group additionally caters to high-end customers who are willing to pay for the best doctors and the best services. All four hospitals have international accreditation and actively promote their services abroad to other countries in Southeast Asia and the Middle East.

A second focus is agents, such as insurance and medical tourism agents. "We have business to business (B2B) clients: business owners, factory owners who want their employees to be taken care of. We also need to attend to the universal coverage that we as a private hospital need to support".

Remarkably, the Group has never really experienced rough financial times, such as those experienced by its competitors in the 1997 Southeast Asian financial meltdown, a crisis that spurred competitor, Bumrungrad, to explore medical tourism. "Our customer base, which was sixty percent universal coverage B2B and business to consumer (B2C) areas, saved the day".

But that is not to say it is immune to other externalities, she said. "Our critical change will involve passing the business from the first to second generations. And I think that's about to come".

Funding the Expansion

While the source of funding differed for each branch of the group, the overall approach to growth was to commence with renting a space, building a name, followed by reputation building. As stated earlier, the first polyclinic saw the owners rent the land. But by the time of the third and fourth hospitals, the Group began to own the land as well as the buildings, and had started to purchase additional land in anticipation of future growth in those locations.

The former "4 branches of Srivichai Hospitals" were rebranded in 2011 as the "Vichaivej International Hospital Group" when entering Thailand's stock exchange market in 2012. With over five hundred in-patient bed capacity altogether, the Group focuses on public health support to international standards, and provides a 24-hour medical service with specialist physicians and specialised treatments. It has more than 2000 pharmacists, nurses, and staff supporting its one hundred consultants.

In the early days, ownership of the Group's first hospital, The Srivichai Yaek Fai Chai, became problematic. Conflicts had begun to emerge and ownership moved from Pyn's mother and father and the generals to include a family member, who was subsequently not allowed to invest in the remaining hospitals due to differing views. Given that ownership often comes with differing expectations and timelines, trying to accommodate the needs and horizons of multiple investors was a challenge.

Interestingly, three or four years after the public listing, the family member who had purchased the hospital said she couldn't do it anymore. "She was getting old, lacked the capital for further development and didn't have a team", continued Pyn. "All the generals had remained with my father and mother, so she sold the company back to our mother company".

Expansion continued with the opening of a second hospital, the Srivichai Hospital Nongkhaem, which was rebranded as the Vichaivej International Hospital Nongkhaem in 2011. In common with the first hospital, the Group also rented the land for the hospital, inviting the owner of the land to become a shareholder. They also recruited shareholders. The hospital offers similar clinical services to Vichaivej International Hospital Omnoi, and has around two hundred beds. Considered the most modern hospital in Thonburi, it operates according to international standards and provides services to foreign clients. Marketing has been promoted in several countries in Asia and the Middle East.

"For the third and fourth hospitals", said Pyn, "we learned from our experience with the first and second hospitals that the best way was to own everything", she said. "Because we didn't own the land, it meant there were limitations on the space that in turn limited the number of projects my father was pursuing".

The third hospital, Vichaivej Hospital, Omnoi, is located in Samutsakhon. Its main customers comprise two major groups: individuals, workers compensation, and foreign customers, and a second group of patients under social security funded programmes, those under the Universal Health Care Coverage Project, and those under foreign labourer health insurance projects. There are plans, she said, to attract private companies, factories, educational institutions; life insurance companies; civil servants and their family under the Diagnosis-Related Group (DRG) project, as well as foreign patients residing in Thailand, whether as tourists or working in the country.

The third and fourth hospitals are situated around forty kilometres outside Bangkok, where the land bank is less restrictive. This means, she said, that you can buy a piece of property out there and have free reign to expand and do all the things you wanted.

A decision was made to open a fourth hospital, Vichaivej International Hospital Samutsakorn; the one hundred-bed hospital is situated on a large parcel of land owned by the Group, although land use still remains quite restrictive. It is the first private hospital in Thailand and the only one in Samutsakorn province that has been selected to participate in the health insurance scheme for migrant workers. Located in an industrial area densely populated with migrant workers, it offers similar comprehensive clinical services as that of Vichaivej International Hospital Omnoi. It also has a clinic at Mae Sot District, Tak Province, that serves Thai and Myanmar customers, and has cooperative agreements with partners in Myanmar for foreign worker health in Yangon.

Fresh Funds, Future Opportunities

The fresh funds generated from the listing paved the way for future projects. Although her father no longer practices, he and his wife remain enthusiastic about investment possibilities, a prospect that sees him traveling to Myanmar, Cambodia, and Laos. Her mother, she said, remains at home as CEO to "rule the generals".

The Group has invested in hospitals in the region and has established a company connection in Cambodia as well. "We are trying to grab this opportunity and put our network into the connecting districts, which will see foreigners from various countries able to travel to Thailand".

Pyn and her father visited Mae Sot in the north-west corner of Thailand, where the Group's networking hospital, Nakhon Mae Sot International Hospital (MSI), is located. She told her father that the hospital looked promising. "All that was needed was a little bit of marketing to attract everyone in the area".

Mae Sot, she said, is home to many wealthy people and has a growing economy. It also forms the main gateway between Thailand and Myanmar, connecting the AEC to Southeast Asian countries, which enables the Group to service clients in Myanmar as well as Thailand. Previously, if Mae Sot residents wanted to reach medical services, they needed to cross the mountains, a trip of more than seventy kilometres.

The Group went on to network with the fifty-nine-bed Nakhon Mae Sot International Hospital (MSI), the only international hospital in the region. International hospital accreditation is an important consideration. "If you are only accredited as meeting Thai standards, you can't take care of foreign patients. You need staff that is able to communicate with international patients. We hired a ten-member Burmese-speaking employee team".

Family Ties

The youngest of four children, Pyn said her father tried hard to convince her to become a doctor. It was the dream of her parents: her eldest sister is a dermatologist, her second sister is a paediatrician, and her brother is an orthopaedist. "I had big fights with my dad as well. But I am the youngest. It means I'm the rebellious one. However he always told us to have our own desires and go for it". The problem was, she added, that he expected that we wanted just what he wanted".

However her mother asked her not to be a doctor. "Do a business degree please and come and help me". After graduation, Pyn spent three years with the Group before joining the Masters in Marketing (MIM) programme at Thammasat University.

The programme expanded her knowledge, enabled her to meet different people, and develop a number of friends, including her future husband, who proved to be very entrepreneurial-minded, she said. The couple graduated and went on to develop an e-commerce platform.

"I actually learned to do things for myself for the first time". This was in contrast to her time as marketing assistant at the hospital where her subordinates saw her as the daughter of the owner. "I didn't get to do much".

While her father wanted her back in the family enterprise, he knew better than to ask her directly to come back. Ever the strategist, he invited her to visit the hospitals in the provinces and neighbouring countries, after which he would seek her input. Pyn agreed to the idea and went on to survey three hospitals and staff.

Not to be outdone by her father's wily approach to getting her back into the family business, she told her father that if he truly wanted her back, he would be able to answer three questions:

Firstly, "Do you think you have a problem with this investment (that they had just viewed)? If you already think that it's good, then you won't need anyone, so don't ask me".

He responded by saying that he did have a problem. "I am old", he said, "and I am only just a doctor. I don't know about marketing. I've used my gut feeling in the business for the last thirty years. But to be able to compete, not only with Thai people, but also with others in Southeast Asia, then I'm not so sure I can do it. So I think I need someone with marketing skills and experience".

Secondly, "Do you think I have what it takes to be the person you need?" She wasn't confident about his answer. The only time she'd rebelled had been over the question of becoming a doctor. "I cannot trust anyone", her father continued. "But you have my DNA. So you're not going to be dishonest. You've grown up with Vichaivej, like your sisters and brother. So, you're the one I can trust".

Thirdly, "Can you see me as a marketing professional and not as your daughter? Can you separate work and family or personal life?" She asked this because she considered her parents as being unable to separate their work and personal life. He answered in the affirmative.

Armed with the responses, Pyn agreed to return and went on to help set up the hospital system.

Current Challenges, Succession Planning

Figures are not an area of concern for her right now, she said, staffing is, along with the challenge of professionalising the Group, a task that requires a change in thinking at both the recruitment and organisational culture levels.

At present, there are approximately two thousand full-time and part-time staff of which around thirty percent are doctors (full-time and part-time), with nurses comprising another sixty percent, and the balance being administrative or non-medical staff.

Professional management is a crucial step for business continuity for the next generation, she continued. "Human resources drive the patient experience, and people who are called on to produce this experience must be able to contribute a lot as well. Management also needs to support them".

At the organisational level, in spite of their earlier success translating into action the directions of her father and mother, the generals and their traditional rigid management style presented problems. "Subordinates had to follow instructions, a typical Thai cultural attitude. If someone is more senior than me, in terms of both position and age, then that person is always right. And I cannot say anything even though I don't agree with them".

Coaxing creativity, and getting employees to think beyond their previous narrow confines, was hard and probably the biggest challenge for her in the transition from first to second generation. When she returned to the Group for a second time, she had the chance to talk to middle management, lower management, and the staff involved in day-to-day operations. Her solution was to try and fire up their enthusiasm by getting them more involved through employee engagement. "You don't hear many people in Thailand talking this way", she added. "But, if we are going to create the next set of generals, we need the people to feel that they are a part of the team and that this is their home. This was probably easier to do in the early years when everyone was in a single location. As we spread out around the region, we have to go beyond 'sneaker-net'".

"If you are on top, you have to have a strong foundation. You cannot be on top if you don't have a strong foundation. Look at the French Revolution. The higher position you hold, the lower you have to reach. You have to put your heart into every detail. If the people are not into it, the system won't work. They won't do it. So first of all I have to gain their trust and gain acceptance. We needed to develop a sense of ownership and commitment among them".

Part of the Group's stated objectives is to establish an efficient organisational management process and a proper human resources management system that gives priority to every single employee, through creation of a culture that allows a free exchange of ideas and opinions.

As family members move back into the Group, succession planning is an issue to be addressed. Pyn's father is now eighty and her mother is seventy-four. Ten years from now, she does not see her parents in operational roles anymore, although they may have roles as consultants. "My father is a visionary, but he's stubborn. All of them grew up in the production era. But it isn't like that anymore. Now we're in a patient-focused era". There was a time when prompt capacity was a sufficient competitive advantage. But the future will involve delivering an experience that drives consumers to choose Vichaivej.

Her generation, she said, is striving to bring the business to an international level, as well as modifying the systems put in place by the preceding generation, along with ensuring a smooth transition from first to second generations.

A second and related challenge or obstacle to be anticipated is whether or not staff and employees can accept the more professional culture promoted by the second generation and whether they can trust the second generation to offer them security, irrespective of their position in the Group. Each generation will view security differently than the preceding generation, she added.

While succession issues are often overlooked by start-ups because future leaders will be drawn from outside the family, that's not the case with the now public-listed Vichaivej International Hospital Group. The influx of the extended family means succession is still very much a family affair, despite its public-listed status.

Endnotes

1. Faculty of Medicine Siriraj Hospital, Mahidol University, is the oldest and largest medical school, and oldest of any kind of university faculty in Thailand. The faculty is now part of Mahidol University. Founded in 1889, the faculty was run in co-operation with Siriraj Hospital, the first public hospital in Thailand, which provided the students with clinical experience.
2. Thailand Board of Investment, www.boi.go.th.
3. Thomson Reuters Tax & Accounting, "Thailand Introduces Special Economic Zones", 15 January 2016, https://tax.thomsonreuters.com/blog/onesource/thailand-introduces-special-economic-zones/.

Chapter 4

DRINKING IT IN: SAPPE'S SUCCESS EMPHASISES INNOVATION AND SHAPING ITS INNO CULTURE

The transition of Sappe, a Thai food and beverage company with a global presence, from a small-scale traditional Thai snack manufacturer reflects a constant striving for innovation and the desire of the founders to enter the new sectors. When one of their sons attended a food science conference, it provided the inspirational springboard for the move, in spite of a relatively small marketing budget. The firm has since entered the growing health and beauty beverage sector, where it has continued to prosper in a very short space of time, eventually listing on the Stock Exchange of Thailand in 2014. In fact, Chief Operating Officer, Arnupap Ruckariyapong, emphasises the importance of public listing and the building blocks of its new culture to the sustainability and success of third, fourth, and future generations.

Thai beverage manufacturer Sappe has been focused on satisfying health-and beauty-conscious consumers for some years, transitioning from a traditional snack manufacturer that commenced operations in 1973. At that time, the first generation Anan Ruckariyapong, who was passionate about making desserts, bought a small oven to bake traditional snacks at home and then sold them at various outlets at train stations and bus terminals. The leading product, called 'KrongKrang', was a traditional crunchy and salty

Thai snack. Soon after, the 'Piyajit' brand (named after his daughter) was born, and proved immensely successful. At the same time, the small business also bought and sold local snacks on behalf of other small-scale producers, and expanded to rural areas. In 1988, he opened the Sapanan General Food Co. Ltd. in the Bang Chan industrial estate.

Chief Operating Officer, Arnupap Ruckariyapong, joined his parents business just as he was about to graduate. He observed that the traditional snacks produced by the business were not suitable in the growing modern retail market. "Even though the business had been established for quite a while, most of our trade was in the local market and utilised the 'mom and pop' store concept as a sales and distribution channel". It was a prescient observation as modern retailing was rapidly taking over the Thai retailing landscape and general trade in particular.

Impacted by the 1998 Southeast Asian financial crisis, the Thai retailing landscape underwent a significant change that saw the emergence of what is known as modern retailing, which proved a significant move away from the traditional 'mom and pop' outlets operating in general trade in local neighbourhoods. By way of comparison, there were over 400,000 mom and pop outlets in 2004, but by 2014, this figure fell to 280,000, while several modern retail outlets, such as 7-Eleven and Family Mart, opened thousands in this period.

A key milestone for the business at this time was its entry into 7-Eleven, he said. "They had 1,200 shops about three years after I joined in 2005. Now there are more than 9,600".

A particular challenge for small businesses is that the modern trade is very large and well organised and will demand promotional support such as a stocking fee, or 'slotting allowance', to ensure their efforts to stock any new products will not be in vain. They will also insist on market development funds to help develop the product locally, and in some cases, a failure fee to cover lost revenue in case a new product comes in and is unsuccessful. Breaking into modern retail channels is not necessarily an easy matter. "When you're small, they ask quite a lot, but when you're big, your bargaining power is big and fees can be reduced. It's one of the key barriers to launching a consumer-based business. You can have a good idea and product, but you still have to fight all these listing fees and so on". Reinventing the traditional snack products for the new modern market was a tall order, he said.

On the Move from Dry Snacks to Beverages

The move to beverages began to take place in 2002, and reflected his father's long-term interest in the sector. "Ultimately we decided to quit the snacks business around 2010 and make more beverages, even though the snacks were selling quite okay. The future was in the beverage business", he said. Another factor was that the traditional Thai snacks could not be made with machines, and producing snacks also took up a lot of space in the factory.

Arnupap recalled the beverage journey. "My older brother was the first person in the family to join the company from my generation. I had just graduated and my mother wanted me to do my Masters' degree right away. But I was afraid it might be too late to take advantage of changes in the industry. We made the decision that my older brother would help first and I would continue and study for my Masters'".

His brother later attended a food science conference at Kasetsart University, a public research university in Bangkok, and discovered

Nata de Coco, a chewy, translucent, jelly-like food with high fibre produced by the fermentation of coconut water that lends itself to a variety of desserts and drinks. "Nata de Coco Drink was our first product launched in 2002, and we were the first one in the world to put Nata de Coco into beverages". When the beverage business commenced, he said, they employed a food technologist who advised about the food process, but not the equipment side. "We never had anything to do with beverages. It was a different game altogether". The nitty-gritty of the business was done in-house, he said. "In the beginning, a lot of it was trial and error, but we learned".

His older brother, who came up with the Nata de Coco idea, graduated from Nagoya University in Japan and after working for a Japanese company, he returned to Thailand to join the business. His sister, a graduate from the University of Sheffield in the United Kingdom, came back to Thailand to work in the banking sector and also joined the business a few years before its public listing. Nowadays, Adisak Ruckariyapong is chairman of the executive committee, and his sister, Piyajit Ruckariyapong, is chief executive officer.

The good thing about the diversification into beverages, Arnupap said, was that the business already had a building, although it was yet to develop into a proper factory building. "When I first joined the company, I was always stressed every time it rained heavily because it meant something or the other would go wrong. It could be either flooding in the factory or an electrical failure somewhere. But we did have a facility".

Back in the snack-making days, the business did not have the proper equipment, and products were made in the kitchen in contrast to the beverage production line, which was state-of-the-art and custom-made.

However, as he freely admitted, the family had no experience in beverages. And while the product was well-received and sales volumes were quite high, there were problems. Products were returned, which was stressful. "We didn't know how to maintain and preserve the product quality as well as we can today".

Retaining customers throughout this period proved to be challenging. "We didn't really sit down with the customers. But my dad has a very long history and relationship with the buyers and is very honest and straightforward. Even though the amount was quite large, we were able to refund the customers in a timely manner for the problems that occurred in the beginning".

Standardisation was the solution, he said, and major changes were afoot. The earlier quality pitfalls had seen the company emphasise quality control to meet set standards, starting from sourcing to procurement through to the entire production process. Sappe now holds various accreditations: Hazard Analysis and Critical Control Points (HACCP), a systematic measure to ensure food safety that can be used at all stages of a food chain, from food production and preparation processes including packaging and distribution; ISO 9001, a standard of quality management systems, that also demands involvement by upper executives in order to integrate quality into the business system; Good Manufacturing Practices (GMP Codex), the practices required in order to conform to guidelines provide requirements that a food product manufacturer must meet to assure that the products are of high quality and do not pose any risk to the consumer or public. It also holds Halal and Kosher certifications to ensure compliance with Muslim and Jewish dietary requirements, as well as meets the requirements of the Food and Drug Administration of Thailand.

Welcome to Sappe Playground

The commitment to innovation sits behind the aim to create Thai brands that can be taken around the world, says Arnupap. "Innovation was the key to success for our differentiated thinking to wow the consumers of our products". It is now endorsed at every possible point throughout the business and is a key success factor, reflected in the office layout as well as its corporate culture. The sign on the front door to the open plan office, for example, says, "Welcome to Sappe Playground". The conference room is set up like bleachers at a sporting event, and is a place for town hall meetings among other events, with cushions to sit on rather than upright chairs. Other rooms have catchy names and dedicated purposes: the "Speed Room", for example, where no meeting can exceed thirty minutes, and the "InnoStudio" room, where innovations are to take place and where "Have the courage to say no to good ideas" is top-of-mind.

The company's corporate inno culture promotes three pillars of innovation. The first is the mind-set of the people, he said. A second pillar relates to the process. "'Dare to dream, play to win' is one way to put it. It's how we do things cross-functionally or within the functional teams themselves, how they make it creative, dynamic, and fun for people to work together and come up with new ideas all the time". The third and last pillar is the "Inno Studio" where funding is intended to support new innovative projects in a fast track lane, whether they be process improvement, business models that it wants to explore, or a new category or new research. "Inno Think" is an internal competition where employees submit their ideas for new products and innovations within the organisation. The winning team gets some incentive from the revenue of the new innovation for one year. It's a significant motivator for employees to come up with new ideas. "Going through a pitch process helps you build better ideas. People become more aware of what they do within an organisation". The company also sets aside a certain percent of top-line revenue for innovation.

Arnupap believes that Thai people, whatever their background, have potential, "but sometimes they don't have a good environment". The commitment to innovation is one way to change this. "Our core belief is that Thai people have a lot of skills, benefits, and advantages but it's untapped. So we need to unleash that".

Sappe, the Innovative Spirit

In 2013, the business changed its name to Sappe Public Company Limited as part of its move to becoming an internationally recognised brand. Listed on the Stock Exchange of Thailand in 2014, Sappe seeks to be a leader in the innovative beverage industry, offering consumers quality products with a twist, differentiated, and outstanding consumer values. Products now go all over Thailand, with a majority exported. "Our goal right from the beginning was to establish an international presence for a Thai brand", said Arnupap. "We're on the way there but not quite there yet. In some countries, people know our brand. But in a lot of countries, we're just still starting. So we need to continue that mission".

Sappe employs 700 staff including outsourced employees, and places great emphasis on the well-being of employees. "We believe that if our employees enjoy their work then they will be able to excel, allowing us to move our company forward together".

In the early stages of production, Sappe had a small marketing budget and effectively had no real competition. "After we became popular in the first eighteen months, there were eleven local brands trying to come up with the same features", he said with reference to Sappe's first product, the Nata de Coco drink.

"We also knew we had a long way to go before we could become a well-recognised brand, so we focused on every single detail of the production process. We wanted all our products to be known for their quality, knowing that quality will market itself".

Similarly, market research was on the back burner in the early days. "Market research was not as extensive as today. Before, we just did our best to differentiate. We were trying to do something that isn't already in the market. Differentiation was our key competitive advantage because we didn't have the money, skills, and know-how at that time. We only had a product that was different".

Taste determines the uniqueness of the product, he said. "We're very strict on the taste. It's checked at least five times. Likewise, the management has constantly monitored and improved the production and texture of the coconut jelly, which makes it more of a superior offering. We have also kept up with the evolution of Mogu Mogu (a juice drink with Nata de Coco cubes inside) over the years as the unique juice with chewing that leads to an extraordinary fun experience".

Sappe's Portfolio and its Forthcoming Journey

Following the success of Mogu Mogu, the company in 2006 introduced a brand new health beverage known as the Sappe Beauti Drink, promoted as the beauty you can drink. This was in line with the demands of the Thai market, which placed great importance on functional benefits to enhance beauty. The beauty drinks were collagen-based drinks, and included SKUs with fibre and other functional ingredients added. They started to be known as "functional drinks", a new category of health drink that catered to beauty-loving Thai women. Collagen, for example helps improve tired-looking skin, while a high amount of fibre helps with digestion.

Sappe Beauti Drink quickly rose to the top spot without mass marketing. The benefits of the drink spread by word of mouth, making it the number one functional drink in Thailand. The product emphasised the quality of raw materials and ingredients. In the functional beverages category, Sappe still holds the highest market share in the Thai women's segment, providing beauty and health benefits to supplement normal diets. Products include Sappe Beauti Drink, Sappe Beauti Shot, and St. Anna. In 2009, Beauti Drink won the "taste09" Innovative Award at ANUGA, the world's leading food fair and retail trade held in Germany — proving that innovations from Thailand could be competitive in the global arena.

Currently, Sappe products are available on the domestic and export markets, focusing on four main categories, namely functional beverages, fruit juices, functional powders, and ready to drink products (RTD). Looking at their product array, it is obvious that the innovation team is hard at work.

Sappe's subsidiary, the All Coco Group, is another business model that generates quite a unique contribution to the Sappe portfolio. All Coco holds one of the largest networks of NAM HOM coconuts, the Thai breed famous for its taste and quality worldwide. NAM HOM can only be grown from the four provinces of Thailand where the soil is rich and has specific characteristics that make it taste the way it should. Like Sappe, the All Coco Group too was created from product innovation and creativity. Now, All Coco offers a franchise business model for its all-about-coconut café's value-added product portfolio made from NAM HOM, such as HPP coconut water, coconut pudding, coconut ice cream, coconut slushies, etc. With All Coco, Sappe is able to generate a new kind of value-added business model in addition to its existing portfolio of innovative products.

A 2018 first quarter snapshot of company sales shows that Sappe has grown considerably from its home market Thailand (at 31 percent), to Asia (more than 47 percent), the European Union and the United States (9 percent) and the Middle East and others (13 percent). Not bad for what was a Thai snack maker a decade earlier with a more diversified portfolio, who stepped back to its roots of snack, for instance, the launch of BeautiJelly, as well as two more healthy snacks, in 2018.

Diversification of the Sappe portfolio has led to success and sustainable growth. Today, Sappe's brands are available in mainstream channels in over 80 countries, with about 200,000 outlets around the world. The assortment of products in different emerging categories will be the next challenge of Sappe to further leverage its distribution and enable differentiation of its portfolio in each region. All in all, it is the speed to innovation, that can capture the latent needs of consumers with the right products, and business models that has taken Sappe where it is today.

On the Challenges of Going Public

The first major challenge, said Arnupap, was the inability to find a successful model. "I still believe that the most important principle is the product. That's how we actually grow the company. We will fail if we cannot come up with products that innovatively meet the needs of consumers all the time. We might be a public company but compared to a Nestle or Coca-Cola, we're just a tiny speck. We don't want to compete with them. Our key challenge is to create a 'passionate twist to life' for our consumers around the world".

As many of the ideas emanated from the family itself, a potential challenge is to synthesise the ideas from the collective organisation. In this respect, the transition to a public listed company is sometimes hard to do for family businesses. "We try hard not to be a one-man show. We were not sure how to innovate systematically. By that I mean we wanted to try to create a system that's able to innovate by itself even if some of the key people are not here. Of course, we don't want them to leave, but the organisation itself has to be able to move forward and innovate with its own ecosystem. So this is one of our challenges. It's a real trial and error. We want to try. Of course we don't want to make any mistakes, but if we do, then we will fix it fast".

Going public was a seminal revelation. "I attended a seminar for second- and third-generation family businesses. My key takeaway here was that if you want to be successful in later generations, you need to go public. Let's say for the third and fourth generation and so forth. In Thailand and other countries, you see a lot of infighting within families over business and things like that. We don't want that to happen".

Arnupap emphasises that it's not the company's main purpose to gain benefit from the stock market, a viewpoint that may differ from that of other corporations. Its main reason for making profits is business-related, he said. In his opinion, shares do not really create additional value; the point is to be able to meet the shareholders' expectations. "We should not just look at short-term profit. We have to build the business long term. It is what allows us to sustain our competencies in the long run that counts".

Despite its manufacturing competence and creative inno culture, Thailand has created few recognisable international brands. But the past decade has seen the emergence of this food & beverage player far beyond the borders of the land of smiles. It will be interesting to see what the next decade brings.

SECTION 2: The Female
Founders: The Power of Mom

Entrepreneurship comes in all sort of shapes and sizes — home spun businesses, international outreaches, importing or exporting of ideas or cultures, food, fashion technology — it is hard to predict what the winners will be. The opportunities and the businesses that are created are truly diverse. But, for many avid business readers, they think of entrepreneurs as driven, hardnosed, competitive risk takers that throw caution to the wind and pursue their economic dreams. The hunters of society, there is a general default expectation that the vast majority of these businesses will be started and run by men.[1]

But, that is not the case in Thailand, as female entrepreneurs are both common and prevalent. A 2005 study conducted by Minniti, Arenius, and Langowitz reported that Thai females had the highest rate of participation in entrepreneurial activity across 35 high and medium income countries over 5 continents.[2] Furthermore, the Grant Thorton study on female representation in Senior Management positions in 2011 found Thailand had the highest rate in the world. Today, Thai females are 1.5 times more likely to participate in senior management positions than the worldwide average.

Southeast Asia is home to more than 61 million female entrepreneurs, more than in Europe and the USA combined.[3] Thailand presents a particularly interesting case as it is the only country in the world where both nascent and established female business owners outnumber their male counterparts.

As you read the next two stories, it should be easy to understand how and why this is the case. The power of mothers can often overcome insurmountable odds and obstacles thought to be impossible to scale. Building trust was vital to the success of Lamoon, Thailand's leading organic baby care manufacturer, which was established by a group of alumni from Thammasat University's MIM program. Created by a new mother with a son suffering from a painful skin allergy, the four founders were not bound by family ties but by a mutual concern for the care of their children. Product lines emphasise continuous quality innovation and are much sought after by parents-to-be and new mothers. Lamoon's success is an inspiring one, especially at a time when similar global outlets are in process of closing.

In the case of the well-known Waraporn Steamed Buns Shop, founder Khun Waraporn Suthanya was running a small corner store when her husband, a fishmonger at the local wet market, was about to lose his stand at the market. Faced with a looming family financial crisis, she cooked. Word-of-mouth, a powerful marketing tool, saw this small-scale enterprise metamorphose into Waraporn Salapao, the ubiquitous steamed bun chain now found across Thailand.

Endnotes

1. Caroline Hatcher, Siri Terjeson & Max Planck, "Towards a New Theory of Entrepreneurship in Culture And Gender: A Grounded Study of Thailand's Most Successful Female Entrepreneurs", 2007.
2. Minniti, Allen, & Langowitz, "The Global Entrepreneurship Monitor study of entrepreneurs identified the emerging patterns of participation of women", 2005.
3. Women's entrepreneurship Conference Bangkok 2017, http://www.women-entrepreneurship.org/.

Chapter 5

LAMOON: WHEN CARING MOMS INNOVATE

Lamoon, Thailand's leading organic baby care brand, reversed the traditional business model and made a successful transition from a formidable online presence to physical bricks and mortar outlets, including designer boutiques. Lamoon means "soft and gentle" in Thai, and its product lines emphasise continuous quality innovation and are much sought after by parents-to-be and new mothers. Yet few consumers outside Thailand know the brand's backstory. Created by a new mother with a son with a painful skin allergy, assisted by three of her classmates from Bangkok's Thammasat University's Master's in Marketing (MIM) program, Lamoon's success is an inspiring one, especially at a time when similar global outlets are in the process of closing.

Like many skincare innovations, including the secrets of legendary maestros like Helena Rubenstein and Elizabeth Arden at the dawn of the twentieth century, necessity is forever the mother of innovation. When Lamoon Managing Director, Nednaphit Rungthanakiat, saw her baby son in pain from a severe skin allergy, she knew she had to find a solution. "He was allergic to detergent, salts, lotions, and skincare products, as well as milk and eggs. It was heartbreaking to watch him struggle". As many parents are aware, allergies like these are not uncommon. Worse, many of the baby products available in the market at that time used chemicals, which exacerbated his condition. "I brought him to see many doctors, but all they did was prescribe steroids. I don't think that was right. We can only use steroids for seven days. Any longer and it affects the baby's skin".

A previous product development manager with Nestle and 7-Eleven, Nednaphit Rungthanakiat, better known as Ying, knew where to start and her quest for a solution began in earnest. "I was looking at making something organic that was one hundred percent natural. As far as I could see, it was a case of changing the soap. The Internet helped me to look around the world for ingredients that were chemical free. I brought them together and created my own soap for my son. It worked and the rashes disappeared. Then I shared my success story with my friends on Facebook".

As her son's skin improved, her friends began to clamour for the soap. The soap was not made at home, although Ying co-formulated the formula with a friend who manufactured it. "We weren't intending to market it", she emphasised. "It was just for my child".

Her friends, a group of four women who met in 2004 during their studies at Thammasat University's MIM program, further developed the soap in late-2007 and early 2008, just after graduation, and established the venture in 2011. The idea came from coursework during the degree programme, where the four discovered an unmet need in the market: most baby products are chemical-based products. "We thought of ourselves as a housewives gang and we were focused on the people we love first, our kids. This became our golden rule. We made the soap to solve a problem and I think that became a form of energy for us".

At first Ying gave the soap away. But she got to a point where she could no longer do that and she set a price and sold it. "My colleague, Piyavadee Liangkobkit, who is now our Sales and

Marketing Director, told me that if it was going to be like this, why don't we produce this as a brand? It's a gift from nature that we can offer to kids experiencing the same problem".

Founders and team members come from complementary backgrounds. Piyavadee Liangkobkit, for example, worked for Kimberly Clark, which saw her bring skills that included ten years of strong professional skills in marketing, trade marketing, sales, and knowledge of Fast Moving Consumer Goods (FMCG), and how to market them in the market place, specifically in the personal care, skincare category. More importantly, said Piyavadee, "All of us share a similar passion".

Supply Chain Director, Jirayu Sommart, worked as a buyer for Unilever, with many years of experience in searching and selecting the ingredients, raw materials, and packaging — all skills that helped Lamoon develop its top five products with a premium quality in very short period.

Meanwhile, Financial Director, Pornpimol Lertmahakit, a chemical engineer, had worked with a trading company that sold spare parts to industry, as well as had many years of experience in entrepreneurship management and emphasised that from her perspective, starting a business was not about selling a product but about identifying the market, validating its size and potential, and then establishing a sound business. "It is vital to understand the big picture of doing business", she said. "What would happen if floods happened? You need to learn how to swim too".

All four reiterated that the business was not formed with making money in mind and was more like a corporate social responsibility (CSR) project, "A benefit to mothers and fathers who were dealing with a problem with their children and to give them a healthy alternative", said Ying.

Mutual trust is important to all four. "You cannot do it all by yourself. You must believe in your team. We all have our own strengths and we lead in our areas of expertise. Regardless of the solution to the problem, we would respect the leader's decision and trust her to lead us into the right direction", explained Ying. Or as Jirayu Sommart noted, "At the end of the day, we are like a chair with four strong legs that couldn't balance without one another. Each person in the team is equally important".

'Mom Insights'

One year after the release of its first five products, the trends and feedback were positive. More and more new customers were added every day. Ying's 'mom-insights' were a key success factor. "I had been working selling baby products such as diapers, baby soap, and wipes. My friend was working in Johnson & Johnson. But as you probably know, there are no real moms working in marketing, some are not even married, which makes it difficult to get any real insights about what the market has and what the market needs".

At this stage, Ying was the only one of the four with children, a serendipitous moment that provided her with 'mom-insights.' "Take cleansers", she said. "Moms are concerned about bacteria and disease. But, what I wanted was something that was also safe for my baby".

Like many mothers, Ying had been using a well-known brand which might kill everything, but was also chemical-heavy, she said. "I didn't think it was safe for my baby because I used it to clean his toys, after which he would just put them in his mouth. So I focused on finding something natural that can reduce bacteria. I found a natural extract that is used to wash fruit and can kill bacteria, as well as being safe for babies when they swallow".

Launched in 2011, Lamoon Baby was the company's first product range, offering organic baby and baby-related products, with one hundred percent natural ingredients, gentle enough for new-born skin and all skin types, with no chemicals, no fragrance, and no parabens. In the beginning, the friends raised US$8,000 to seed the business, focusing first on online sales via Facebook. Today, Lamoon is the market leader in organic care products. "We aim to be a premium brand that targets modern working mothers who care deeply for her little ones", said Ying. "And I am proud to say we are already successful in terms of brand awareness and are now ready to take it to a new level, we are looking at exports".

Over the years, product innovations have included an organic baby accessories cleanser, a body and hair wash gel, hand sanitizer spray, and an organic cotton baby blanket woven from organic cottons, non-chemically grown and processed, organic baby wet wipes, organic baby lotion, as well as making products specifically for mothers such as breastfeeding covers and anti-stretch marks creams.

With each day and each launch, the demand continues to grow. The company recently launched a new set of mosquito repellent stickers for children that were effective at repelling bugs but gentle enough that the child could even ingest them. The group produced what they thought would be enough product for the quarter, only to sell out of product in 48 hours.

Designer Collaborations, Celebrity Endorsements, and Partnerships

After Lamoon began to sell online, sales went up. A turning point took place when a Thai celebrity used the products for her child. Later when another celebrity was about to give birth, the company sent a Lamoon gift basket of organic products, which the new mother promptly posted on her blog. "Back in those days there was no Instagram, just blogs", said Ying.

The strategy worked. Gradually word spread about the new products. "Customers sent us feedback, before and after photos of their babies with a rash that had cleared up. This meant consumers had started to believe in our product", she added. In two years from its establishment, Lamoon achieved its targets, with sales growing one hundred percent. Although still online, the company was now distributing products in the upscale Siam Paragon Department Store and Central Department Store of Bangkok.

Reflecting on the success of the brand, Ying considered three factors beyond performance that helped drive the product's visibility and acceptance. Celebrity endorsement was one, believability another, and a series of innovative partnerships as third. A fourth was its ability to engage its consumers.

"Our branding strives to be different from others", said Ying. "It's not only about the brand story. We try to link it with fashion, which saw us forge a cooperation with Kloset, a well-known Thai designer to make stylish breast feeding covers — Lamoon × Kloset".

Thai fashion company, Kloset, was founded by young fashion designer, Mollika Ruangkritya, and is famous for its craftwork that features hand-made stitching, lace, ribbons, and patchwork. Featured in Vogue Japan, it was a logical partner for Lamoon's young trendy mothers. Ying commented that most of the breastfeeding covers on the market at that time were not fashionable. "The Kloset breastfeeding covers make moms feel better when they have to breastfeed all the time. I wanted mothers to feel like 'okay, come on, I'm still beautiful. I can use a beautiful cover like this.' And when they feel good with our brand, then they will use another product for their baby".

It was an innovative move and had never happened before in the baby market, said Ying, even with Johnson & Johnson and other big brands. "We decided to do this because we want to be different, and different from the run-of-the-mill baby products". The strategy here was to move Lamoon from the baby product sector to a young family lifestyle, which would take up the niche occupied by mothers as well as their babies. Consumers are very happy with the brand, she said.

Other partnerships included Dumex, part of the Danone Group, which has been supplying infant and baby powdered milk in its operations in Thailand since 1957. Another partnership was with Philips AVENT, a healthcare brand with a wide range of products for mothers and babies.

Consumer engagement has remained at the forefront of the company's business model and Lamoon's Outreach programme includes activities for Lamoon families, including collecting recommendations from fathers as well as mothers.

The Challenges

While Ying's mom insights proved useful in driving innovation, there were many roadblocks along the way. "Competitors were always trying to complain about us. But I didn't want to give up. Most of them were just after profits because they saw that we had set the price point high. However the real reason for the high prices was the quality of the ingredients, products, and design".

First among the roadblocks was the effort needed to introduce organic baby products as a mainstream consumer offering. "Even the government questioned the meaning of 'organic'", said Ying. "It was quite hard for me to get the Thai Food and Drug Administration

(FDA) to classify the items as organic products as there were no regulations governing this category at that time. In the end, I had to issue the certificates for them and educate the government staff and consumers about organic products and why they have to be priced higher than other products".

Shelf life was a close second. "Initially we did not put any chemicals and preservatives in our product. This resulted in a very short shelf life for some products. So if we sold the product in a supermarket or in a department store, there would be returns. Therefore we had to reformulate the products with a two-year shelf life in mind", she said.

This hurdle caused Ying to search for one hundred percent natural ingredients as a preservative. Not only were the costs prohibitive, but sourcing the ingredients was hard to do even in Thailand. However, she persisted, remaining true to her beliefs, although it meant spending around two years on the formulation. "Most people told me, 'Come on, it could be ninety-five percent, that's good enough', but I said no, Lamoon has to be one hundred percent natural". The ingredients were found and a small lot produced.

The next challenge was the search for possible manufacturers to make sure they were aligned with Lamoon's goals and passions. As the initial quantity ordered would be small, Lamoon also needed to have a good relationship with the prospective manufacturer. "At that time, we could not follow any Minimum Order Quantity (MOQ) requirements due to our limited sales. When you don't have enough volume, a lot of suppliers don't even want to supply you ingredients because you're not selling enough for them to be interested in doing business with you. Getting someone to manufacture your recipe is yet another struggle when you are small". These days, said Ying, Lamoon's rising sales mean it is easier to manage supply as it meets the manufacturer's minimum order requirements.

Further complicating this relationship was the need for Lamoon to keep their manufacturers or supply chain at a distance because it didn't want third parties to have the complete recipe. "Knock-offs became easier", said Ying. "They can either move into your business or offer semi-structured solutions to would-be competitors that want to come into your market".

Competition was another matter. Lamoon does not compete against mass products, and cannot, as its costs are very high, she said. "So that's why we aim for a premium product. Our competition is imported products. That's why we set our prices lower than imported products, but a little higher than local products". The products' positioning as one hundred percent natural origin represented a challenge to competitors who claimed to use only organic products. To counter this, Lamoon created its own shelf display and used branding to create a unique shelf experience. Similarly, establishing credibility was difficult and tricky for a new entrant in the market place, with a very small company, and a brand that was yet to be established.

But it worked and currently Lamoon has distribution at three hundred stores and outlets in Thailand, including top supermarkets, organic and natural supermarkets, as well as online. Online activities account for forty percent of turnover while traditional bricks-and-mortar outlets comprise sixty percent. "New mothers don't have the time to go out shopping, so online is doing well", Ying said.

The Wheel of Life

Lamoon is expecting to develop its brand in Asia within the next three years, building on existing distribution channels to Hong

Kong, Malaysia, Singapore, Cambodia, and Laos. "China is next up", Ying said noting that expansion will need further exploration of the shelf life formulation. "We are trying new ingredients that will extend the shelf life and lower costs due to a higher MOQ".

The four are pragmatic about future expansion. Interestingly, they are also open to acquisition — providing certain requirements are met. "I think we have to study in detail about any company that approaches us", said Ying. "First of all, do they share our same vision, to help the kids? A second is that we will not compromise on the formulation and our quality. Lamoon is like our baby. If we want to let anyone raise our baby, we have to know them better. We have to be very confident that they will raise our baby as best as possible".

Lamoon and its founding team are committed to better health and outcomes for young families. When asked if they ever thought of giving up during their entrepreneurial journey, the response was a mix of tears and amazement as the team stated, "If we would not have made this product, who would have done this for the children and their families". The team clearly takes solace in the testimonials they receive every day from families that have experienced a great improvement in the semi-chronic conditions their children have been living under.

Personally and business-wise, the wheel of life continues for the team. After pursuing organic child focused products, the four women have now started Bloss Natura, a beauty products business that represents the next step up from babies and small children to re-engaging with the active social life demanded of the modern mom. That business has been formed with two new partners, Panward Boonyaratglin and Porntip Skidjai, the two Thai movie stars who began using Lamoon and writing about it on their blogs.

Chapter 6

THE KITCHEN AT WARAPORN SALAPAO: AN ENGINE OF ECONOMIC GROWTH

Thailand's women have long been noted for their entrepreneurial spirit. In the case of the well-known Waraporn Salapao, founder Waraporn Suthanya was running a small corner store. Her husband, a hardworking fishmonger at the local wet market, was about to lose his stall. Faced with a looming family financial crisis, she turned to what traditional Thai moms do best, cook. Used to making the traditional Chinese-style steamed buns, or salapao, for her children to eat after school as a snack, she started to make a few extra for sale in her mom-and-pop store. Her neighbours and their children found the snacks delicious. Even the local bank began to buy them for their special events and regular meetings. Word-of-mouth, a powerful marketing tool, saw this small-scale enterprise metamorphose into Waraporn Salapao, the ubiquitous steamed bun chain comprising 78 outlets making over 50,000 buns a day, now found across Bangkok, with a few stores also outside the city.

Like most mothers the world over, Waraporn Suthanya, was not a chef or restaurateur, but a good, solid family-style cook. Her children, three boys and one girl, loved her cooking, especially *salapao*, the Chinese-style steamed buns that are a popular snack across Asia, although the four of them still used to line up every afternoon after school to buy the exact same buns from a local hawker. Rather like the hot dog in the United States, the buns are considered a typical street food in Thailand. Fillings can be savoury or sweet, with savoury *salapao* usually consisting of barbecued or minced pork, and tasting pretty much the same wherever they are to be found, usually at hawker stalls, roadside eateries, and Chinese restaurants. But there are exceptions, and a winning recipe is always able to pull a crowd from miles around.

Waraporn's own recipe was popular within her family, and she decided to make the *salapao* buns for her children to eat after school as a snack before dinner. Soon she started to make a few extra. The buns proved so popular that she began to make more, which she sold in the multipurpose kiosk that she ran in front of her house. Patrons pestered her to make even more. Even the local bank began buying them for their events and before long, all four children not only walked out the door with their own *salapao* in their schoolbags, but were pressed into delivering the snacks to their mother's customers on their way to school.

The small steamed buns kiosk that had begun trading in 1992 in front of an old house in the Nang Lerng neighbourhood now became a small home enterprise. In those pre-social media days, word-of-mouth saw the bun's reputation grow. People came from other neighbourhoods just to try the buns. It was a serendipitous blessing as the family was struggling financially. The buns provided an opportunity for greater economic prosperity.

The demand continued to grow. Over the next five to seven years, the family ran the shop, people called to order the buns, and the kids continued to deliver the product using a motorcycle taxi service. The business gradually scaled up, and soon there were kiosks or restaurant in many malls and department stores of Bangkok. As to where the energy came from to drive the growth, Poom, her eldest son and current company CEO, said they drew strength from one another. "It was a joint effort involving all of us". Truly a family enterprise, the company has evolved and grown over the years.

A second shop was opened around 2004. It was a fair distance from the original shop, said Poom, the strategy being to follow the burgeoning customer base. "We opened there because there were customers in the area, including the bank that had been a regular patron and existing corporate clients, as well as offices and more potential consumers".

The shop progressed to a small restaurant, with the menu now including more than just buns. Various a la carte dishes were offered, including around twenty kinds of dim sum, as well as rice dishes with red pork, braised pig shank, and baked chicken, along with newer flavours and Zongzi (pyramid-shaped dumplings made by wrapping glutinous rice in bamboo leaves). Although the first outlet offered no seating, by the time the second outlet had opened, they were able to offer limited seating in a space of seventy square meters. And by the time the ninth outlet had opened, Poom said the family knew it had a viable business, "one where the entire family could work together".

If in the early days Waraporn was making around one hundred buns per day, by the time the business had expanded to seventy-eight restaurants and outlets, a dramatic increase in output had taken place. The factory now produces fifty thousand buns per day, or around five hundred to a thousand buns per shop per day. Notwithstanding the volume, the family recipe has remained the same: the buns have not been adjusted to the tastes of each outlet. A crucial element is the nutritional production process plus the flour formula used. "The only changes we have made relate to a longer shelf life", Poom added. "Everything is prepared in the one place in the factory, with the semi-finished product sent to the outlet where it is then heated and sold".

Over the course of more than twenty-five years, the Waraporn Salapao family business has gone from a small steamed bun kiosk to a chain of restaurants and outlets that still sell Waraporn Suthanya's original recipe, its buns being famously "filling as well as soft". A competitive pricing strategy, and restaurant option for a quick lunch or snacks to take back to the office or home, is part of its success, said Poom. With a nod to the present, the calorie value of the buns now appear on apps like My Fitness Pal, and its famous buns and dumplings are featured on Instagram and reviewed on various social media sites. A far cry from the two dozen or so buns being set out on the shop counter still fresh from the mother's stove.

Expansion

Seventy-eight outlets translate to an average opening of one new shop every three months or so since 2004. Sites were selected on the basis of an existing community or village, as well as department stores and malls because they act as a hub for customers. In the malls, some outlets have seating, while some do not and just cater to the take-away segment. Most are located within a 200 kilometre radius from Bangkok. But ultimately, said Poom, "selection of the sites comes down to more of an 'instinct'".

A traditional conservative approach, eschewing banks and finance, was used to underwrite the expansion. "When funds were available, we opened a new store. We were not at the beck and call of the banks. When the money came in, and if there was enough money to open a shop, then we did it", Poom explained. If there wasn't — they waited.

Waraporn Salapao is now looking at entry into the main "up-country" provinces (a term for anywhere outside of Bangkok) across the country, "in Asia too", said Poom. While plans are afoot for a second factory, there is no intention to diversify into a different food concept. "If you change the product concept, it means the people and everything else will have to change".

"Just a Bun" and Other Challenges

In the early days of the business, *Salapao* was usually considered to be cheap street food, selling at around six Baht apiece (roughly 20 US cents). The initial challenge for Waraporn Salapao was to produce a bun of good quality, more than "just a bun", but not as cheap as street food, and not as expensive as the buns found in hotels, said Poom. By 2018 though, their buns were being sold at 22 Baht a bun, and competitors too were pricing it around the same. It was also no longer considered to be street food, and could be found in multiple outlets, such as malls.

A second challenge, he recalled, came in the form of the 2011 floods. Like most Thai businesses, Waraporn Salapao bore the brunt of the massive flooding that took place from July 2011 to January 2012, the worst flooding in five decades, with more than three quarters of Thailand's provinces declared flood disaster zones. The World Bank estimated that the economic loss exceeded US$45 billion. The factory was flooded and outlets were closed for one month. "But we still had to pay the rent", said Poom.

However the change from a family business to a private company was probably the most significant challenge, he said. After all four children went on to earn degrees, they joined the family business, which was run like any other typical Thai Chinese business "with the money in one place", he explained. But as the business expanded, this was unworkable and the decision was made to incorporate the business. "The hardest part was to convince our mother that this would work".

The decision ushered in major changes in the organisation, from working structures, recruitment of more employees, to payments and remunerations that had to meet performance objectives. "All of us (children) are now employees of the company", he said, "a decision that families very often don't like to take". Poom became CEO of the new company responsible for management and overall strategy, a second brother was tasked with finance, the third brother was responsible for the factory and production, while their fourth sibling is now married and has stepped back from the business.

Despite the change, the bun business remains a simple business, Poom said modestly. "It's not really complicated". Many would disagree, citing the fickleness of foodies and a fast moving market place. But thus far, Poom and his siblings have managed successfully to catch that elusive taste tiger by the tail. The name of its founder is still on the door and her family recipe still guides the restaurant's core. Truly the power of a Mom!

SECTION 3: The Start-up Entrepreneur

Family businesses are only a part of the developments in entrepreneurship now taking place in Thailand. Other enterprises are more properly considered start-ups, unsupported by family members and funding, where founders have simply had a 'light bulb' moment, capturing a market need or seizing a business opportunity, and reflecting the changes in society, retailing, and consumer behaviour.

The first case is of Priceza, a Thai price comparison and e-commerce search engine, and is a classic start-up. Founder Thanawat Malabuppa was studying computer science at the same time as the founders of fellow start-up, Wongnai. The introduction of 4G telephony and better mobile devices went on to spark company growth, while the infusion of private equity funding helped professionalise operations as well as aid the company's expansion into Indonesia, Singapore, Malaysia, Vietnam, and the Philippines.

The second, Wongnai, is a lifestyle portal that features over two hundred thousand restaurants, salons, spas, and other information across Thailand on its platform, together with details of each merchant and user reviews. Wongnai is now moving beyond its original focus and exploring other possibilities such as parenting sites and even pet services. CEO and co-founder, Yod Chinsupakul, is exhorting the next wave of Thai entrepreneurs to find their passions and follow their dreams.

The third, At Vantage Co. Ltd., a Thai market research agency, founded by Suttipan Sutas Na Ayuthaya, decided to take on the four major global research giants. When he noticed his profession was increasingly unable to deliver its true potential, he knew it was time for a change. He explored and delivered technology, bringing under the same roof insight teams, software, IT, and analytics groups, and transformed his agency into a leader in market intelligence services.

The fourth, Alto Coffee, a retail and wholesale coffee business based in Bangkok, founded by Patthrapon Ruangsuteerakit ("Tae"), is driven by quality. Tae started off by selling premium grade pasteurised soy milk, but then, as sales did not take off as planned, the business was wound down. He then started a café business in the Central Business District in Bangkok. Three cafes opened in the span of six months and were established to sell the same coffee at different price points, and served as an experimental ground for Tae to understand what consumers liked in their coffee. In 2012, he closed down the three cafes after his initial experiment, and proceeded to open Alto Coffee, an outlet that would sell premium coffee. Tae's goal was to sell premium quality coffee, and he wanted to gain the interest of his customers in the product by educating them about coffee through various touchpoints.

And lastly, when Narindej Thaveesangpanich, the farsighted entrepreneur at the helm of Thai Habel Industrial Co. Ltd. took note of Thailand's growing export market, which includes electronics, the staple of his firm. He used an astute three-pronged sequence of strategies and tactics to focus on "strength from within" to lay the groundwork for the company's future expansion into other countries as well as Thailand itself. His strategy included harnessing Thailand's various Free Trade Agreements, which he said offered intending exporters a variety of benefits and access to markets regionally and internationally.

Chapter 7

PRICEZA: BARGAIN HUNTING #2.1

Priceza, the Thai price comparison and e-commerce search engine, is a classic start-up. Founder Thanawat Malabuppa was studying computer science at the same time as the founders of fellow start-up, Wongnai. Like them, he had already started a company, but he and his two colleagues made the mistake of outsourcing development. The eventual solution was good, but in a fast-changing market, modification and updates were inevitable to adjust the face of the software to the public. Having outsourced IP development, they had a "pretty good solution" that could not be modified. The introduction of 4G telephony and better mobile devices sparked company growth, while the infusion of private equity funding helped professionalise operations as well as aid the company's expansion into Indonesia, Singapore, Malaysia, Vietnam, and the Philippines. Others will follow.

The days of the hot, crowded traditional market, the traders hawking and squawking their wares and the jostling hordes might be long gone in the minds of modern shoppers, but they are not forgotten. In 2018, many of those very same traders now have a social media presence and still carry on their businesses in the virtual market place. With access to new gadgets and mobile phones, holidays, fashion, and snacks are only a click away, it was just a matter of time before enterprising entrepreneurs, this time from Thailand, combined the offer of a limitless range of products and services with a built-in price comparison facility — all from the comfort of a smart phone and an app, wherever that might be.

Priceza is a shopping search engine that helps consumers look for products, deals, and promotions online, and then aggregates them in one place to enable consumers to make the best shopping decision. While it is now a hugely successful enterprise, back in its ideation phase, its three founders only knew they wanted to get into price comparison, but struggled with the venture's first steps. Thanawat Malabuppa, one of the three founders, discusses the evolution of the site and its backstory in this chapter.

Getting Started

The latest model start-ups have attracted major attention from large-scale investors and venture capitalists. But when Priceza commenced operations in 2010, there was low internet penetration in Thailand, 3G and 4G services were yet to commence, merchants were plagued by credit card and bad debt issues, and as if that was not enough, the country was not set up for delivery to the more remote regions. These were daunting prospects for an innovative price comparison site.

Yet within a relatively short space of time, Priceza had been able to log around 7.5 million active users across its website and mobile app in Thailand alone, as well as expand its services to other countries in Southeast Asia, including Indonesia, Malaysia, Singapore, Vietnam, and the Philippines, through multiple languages (Bahasa, English, Tagalog) — transforming itself in the process to meet the demands of the times.

In 2010, when Priceza was launched, the focus of e-consumers and vendors was on price — there were not many other parameters that could be satisfactorily used for comparison. The new site provided consumers of the day with details on price, current promotions, and the best deals currently available, as well as connected the consumer and the seller. "Eight years ago, e-commerce in Thailand was not what you would call e-commerce", Thanawat said, considering a more accurate description of the early model Priceza might be an 'online catalogue' — the only price shown on the website being that of the seller.

The site has evolved. It can now compare many other elements, not just price, using aggregated information to cater to the different interests and needs of the consumers. "One person will want the cheapest and won't care about after-sales service. Others are willing to pay more", he said. "And when payment and delivery options are factored in, it becomes even more complicated. A store might offer the cheapest price, but you need to wait seven days to have it delivered. Another might be more expensive but you can get it within four hours".

Payment options are interesting in their own right. In Thailand, the most popular payment option for e-commerce buyers is currently Cash on Delivery (COD), which, he said, is also the case in the Philippines and Indonesia. "Both countries (the Philippines and Indonesia) unbanked for the most part, with those holding bank accounts under fifteen percent and those with credit cards much lower, and thus prefer to pay on a COD basis". At the same time, vendors and the e-commerce marketplace are impatient when it comes to consumers obtaining credit cards, which sees these merchants offer many kinds of payment options, just to close the sale.

Infrastructure and logistics remain major issues in e-commerce in Thailand and much of ASEAN. In the past, when people wanted to deliver a parcel, they had to rely on the National Thai Postal Service, which was not that good at the time, he said. This changed once private logistics companies moved into the sphere and challenged the services offered by Thailand Post.

"While e-commerce in Thailand currently stands at only eight percent, this is small compared with that of the United States (U.S.) or Japan, where it sits at ten percent, or China where it exceeds ten percent, or South Korea at around sixteen percent". Countries like South Korea and the U.S. have satisfactory logistics and financial infrastructures as well as a preponderance of credit cards, making the e-commerce process easier.

However, to compare e-commerce in the U.S. with Asian consumer behaviour is misplaced, he said. "It is wrong. This is Asia. In the U.S. not many people shop using smartphones. In China, over fifty percent of e-commerce takes place using smart phones. This is also the case in Southeast Asia, especially in Indonesia. Right now, around eighty percent of access to Priceza Indonesia comes from mobile phones. In Thailand, it's around sixty-five to seventy percent".

Successful e-commerce start-ups are catnip to investors, with seven figures — or more — investments mentioned in the deal pages of the financial media in the case of Priceza. Once a successful product and a model are developed, it is relatively easy to replicate. The company's limited resources in the early days led it to make the smallest investment possible to support its activities. It then allowed it to grow organically, ultimately adding more resources. This frugal strategy stands behind the company's successful expansion into Indonesia in 2013, and Malaysia, the Philippines, Singapore, and Vietnam in 2015.

Two basic models are used. The first is the cost-per-click model. "Just like Facebook or Google advertising", he added. The second is the cost-per-sale-commission model. This is minimal, he said. It is around five to ten percent of the overall revenue.

The Click as a Performance-based Objective

Priceza connects the consumer and the seller, with the seller seeking to target and ultimately sell to the buyer. The two groups are matched. If they go to Priceza and buy something, the company earns a certain amount for each click. "However, when the consumer decides not to buy directly from us", said Thanawat, "we send that person to the website of the mobile app of the seller. We collect an advertising fee from each click that we send".

That being said, a sale does not need to take place to make money because it is the size of the traffic that the company will send to the store. Sellers only pay when a click takes place, which sees the click become a performance-based objective. The company painstakingly uploads content from their sellers to the website. In return, they earn no fees for this process. "The click rate is the only revenue source. There's no revenue involved in uploading the information", he explained.

Growth in the company — it had moved into other countries within just 12 months — led the founders to realise there was money to be made not just in clicks, but also in banners and site advertising as the site attracted greater and greater eyeballs.

Priceza sells display or insight by advertising the brands, although this is more like branding awareness, a process where a user can compare many seller options, then compare stores, credit card options, delivery options, and a bottom line price. "This kind of advertising is aimed at driving sales". Additionally, in analysing the clicks and, in some cases, the purchases, the company has a distinct opportunity to offer insights to their online customers.

The Trials of an 'Awesome Product'

The idea for the site emerged when Thanawat Malabuppa, Vachara Nivataphand, and Wirod Supadul, three Chulalongkorn University computer science graduates, thought about starting an internet business.

"We liked the internet. We were trained to write programming and computer software specifications in a very systematic way, which we liked, because a good product has many features. So we researched similar products in other countries such as Japan, the U.S., and Europe. We combined all the features of those countries in one product", Thanawat recalled. "We thought it would be an awesome product".

It took two years of trial and error for the idea to go live on the website. They made many mistakes, he said, which later proved to be significant learning points for them, and probably for other aspiring entrepreneurs. There were too many features on the website software, and they were also unaware of the features needed by Thai consumer. "We did jump in", he acknowledged. "We thought we understood the consumer, but, only a few of those features were really important".

Outsourcing proved another costly learning point.

The three engineers were working full-time and had spent hours and hours after work thinking about the product. Two years went by and the decision was made to outsource the programming behind the core technology to friends. "This was our second mistake. What we learned is that although we needed to outsource the technology, we also needed to understand the core product, how to move it forward, adapt it, and how to organise it".

Outsourcing had its advantages, but as they discovered, it made it virtually impossible to modify or adapt the product, should problems arise — which did, at a later date when the market had evolved.

The big day arrived. The site finally went live, only for it to crash due to a major problem with the software. "We tried hard to fix it but we didn't know what to do because we didn't write the code ourselves and our friend who had written the software was working full-time with another company and could only spend a very small amount of time on the problem", he said. "'It's not our problem. We have finished the coding,' they told me. So, it was actually our problem and we didn't know how to fix it".

When it came to outsourcing, the founders thought they did not need to understand the coding, or the features, or how it works. "We thought we would be the ones to think of the features and the business plan", he said.

Even the business plan proved to be another stumbling block. None of them knew what a business plan was and consulted the internet. "We tried to cover all the topics in the business plan and believed we already had a business", he laughed.

They also believed that many people would use the service from Day 1. Unfortunately, they didn't. But the three of them persevered and decided not to close the business. It was 'running' but not generating revenue; the website remained up.

Realising their limitations, the three went their separate ways and enrolled in Master's degrees. While Thanawat joined the Master in Marketing (MIM) program at Thammasat, Vichara and

Wirod went back to their alma mater and undertook MBAs at Chulalongkorn.

The decision was a sound one, and provided each of them with 'complementary skills'. "What I learned from my MIM was related to market validation", Thanawat said. Another bonus was increased confidence, which fired up his inner sales potential. "I'm an engineer. I didn't think I'd love sales because I'm not the talkative type. But when it was demystified and I understood how to make sales, it became a challenge like any other and I really embraced it".

Validation turned out to be a third learning outcome and a critical point. Previously, the three had not tried to determine whether there was market for the product in Thailand, or even talked to people. Frankly, they had only discussed the idea amongst themselves. Incredibly, he continued, we didn't even talk to the user or the customer. "We are engineers, we were confident we could build something good", he said, rationalising the process.

The second time around, and armed with his new marketing skills, Thanawat began to talk to potential customers and carried out in-depth interviews. One of the potential customers interviewed was the owner of a digital camera shop with an online store and website who gave them some valuable feedback as to what he thought was important.

"He didn't care about the many features we had. What he did care about was the e-commerce website, and the traffic to the site. If we were able to bring him traffic, 'I will pay you money,' he told me. He wasn't concerned about the display either". The camera shop proprietor later became, and remains, a Priceza customer.

The realisation dawned on him that site traffic has to have a direct correlation with revenue: "They're retailers and they want to sell units and have margins on each unit. That's why when we leave their store on our website, we cannot charge them for the display. We only charge them for the clicks because we track performance".

The market validation process confirmed that the two major features needed on the site were the search and price comparison functions.

Genesis

After validation, the earlier venture was scrapped. The new Priceza, launched in 2010, was a slimmed-down version that used the experience gained, tempered with top-up knowledge gleaned from further education. The team now eschewed outsourcing and used just two features. The entire process took only two months compared with the two years of the previous venture, although the three were yet to work full-time with Priceza.

Key success factors were now tabled. The first was the team itself — perhaps the most important. The second was execution. And thirdly, the market itself — the right market as well as the right timing for that market.

The Importance of the Team

Thanawat's observation on the importance of the team transcends the usual motivational management quotes. "Start-ups don't have many assets, especially tech start-ups", he said. As they do not have much in the way of value, the value is in the people who build intangible things, in short, the team.

There was a need to find the right people and ensure they had 'complementary skills.' "Even though the three of us are engineers, I made the decision to focus on the marketing. My other two friends focused on coding and product development", he explained. The teams also need to be able to execute ideas, he added. Products, especially tech company products, have to evolve over time, and if the team cannot evolve, then failure is likely.

"I believe when I look at a business, there are only two core functions: marketing and innovation. As founders, we need to have these two functions, and be dedicated to them".

On Innovation

"Many people think that 'if only I have the idea, I can win, I can get rich from this very big idea!' But this is only a part of the story", he explained. "If you think like that and don't have a team to make it happen or execute it, it won't be successful".

Would-be entrepreneurs, especially in start-ups, need people who can execute the idea and make it happen, is his advice.

The Market

"We started from scratch", he said. "I had to start somewhere so I talked to around thirty e-commerce sellers in the first three months, offering them a free trial in which we would agree to promote their products on our platform for free. After the trial, which was successful, we could then talk further about advertising".

It was one way to get around the lack of stores on the site: "If we don't have the stores, the consumer cannot compare anything. Our basic thought was that if they get put up online for free, they get expanded coverage and the ability to reach whatever crowd goes through our site, for free".

Tracking was the most important aspect of the process: success depended on the click-through rate. Online advertising had to be measurable. "It's numbers-driven. And we won't get paid until we can show them the figures".

It also showed potential customers that the business was growing, which was important down the road when it came to offering advertising contracts.

Growth

By the end of the first year, the team had some revenue but not enough to pay themselves a salary. Those were lean times. All three were still working full-time with other companies, one with Exxon Mobil and the other with Thomson-Reuters, while Thanawat was still working in the family business, which meant he could be more flexible time-wise, working on Priceza in the afternoon.

At the end of 2011, the company started hiring, with Thanawat being the first of the founders to go full-time. Six years later, staffing had grown to almost one hundred and the company now had a small office in Jakarta, Indonesia, employing five to six people.

Investment Inflows

Priceza obtained its first external investment in 2013 from the Japanese firm, CyberAgent Ventures[1]. "Although there were not many start-ups and e-commerce ventures in Thailand in 2012, Priceza was 'among the stars'", he said. "We were on their radar and they approached us". Priceza became CyberAgent's first investment in Thailand.

There were other potential investors as well, including those from Thailand, Singapore, and Russia, but CyberAgent offered the best deal. A tech-focused professional venture capital company, CyberAgent Ventures brought more than funds. It was able to connect with the space, potential customers and partners, and also had investments in Vietnam, Indonesia, Malaysia, and Singapore, as well as Thailand. "In fact, when we expanded to Indonesia, where we didn't have any connections at all, we asked the CyberAgent team in Indonesia to help connect us. And they were able to do that", he said.

Priceza used the Series A funding to expand to other countries as well as invest in people.

In 2016, the German technology and media company-cum-corporate investor, Hubert Burda Media, was seeking to increase its investments in Southeast Asia and approached the company. Given that CyberAgent had planned to exit in around three years, and that the valuation of the company had reached a certain level with no further profit available, it was the right time for them to exit.

Burda Asia CEO, Friedrich von Scanzoni, considered Priceza a natural choice given its growth from an idea in 2010 "to a high-profile platform spanning six countries".[2] At the same time, it also expressed a preference to become the sole investor, which dovetailed in with CyberAgent's planned exit.

Under the Series B funding, Burda Principal Investment acquired a 24.9% stake for a reputed seven-figure amount under which Burda acquired CyberAgent's ten percent holding and agreed to inject fresh operational funds.[3]

Priceza benefited from Burda's Southeast Asia portfolio, as well as its interests in the U.S. and Europe, which brought connections with other companies. Priceza said it would be seeking to build on the connections, develop the synergy among the portfolio companies, as well as leverage Burda's digital expertise and in depth media understanding.

Timeline: "Upward Swings"

Year	Event
2010	Launch of Priceza
	4 million visits
2011	9 million visits
2012	20 million visits
2013	Series A funding (CyberAgent Ventures)
	Launch in Indonesia
	40 million visits
2014	New multiple device platform (mobile phones) launch
	50 million visits
2015	Asia Pacific ITC Alliance Award
	Launch in Vietnam, Malaysia, Singapore, the Philippines
	70 million visits
2016	Series B funding (Burda Principal Investments)
	96 million visits

Further down the line, an Initial Public Offering (IPO) might be in the offing for Priceza, Thanawat said. But it could equally well be a buy-out: "Burda is in media. So if they invest in a company and it grows to a certain level, they could be willing to acquire it as well".

Evolution

Priceza and its e-commerce operations continued to evolve. It began to remonetise the traffic to its site from its earlier click-focused approach to a more detailed and transaction-focused approach that can fully facilitate online advertising.

The company is now able to calculate the number of orders, revenue, return on investment, and cost per order; part of a stream of measurable KPIs that it couldn't have done in the early click days. "Measurability is everything right now", he said, "as it sits behind a client's decision to spend more".

At the same time, Priceza can profile its consumers and store credit card information, both of which enable construction of a tighter segmentation profile by relying on real transactions and not just the ubiquitous cookie in its targeted advertising.

There are many kinds of data points collected, such as clicks, transactions, the kinds of product purchased, the top ten products, and the likes; they also form the basis of the company's e-commerce insights. Details are released at the annual Priceza Awards, an event that enables it to engage with the majority of e-commerce players in Thailand, and an interesting exercise with long-term reputational benefits.

Ultimately it has been an eventful passage for Priceza from a price comparison site that laboured under a surfeit of unnecessary features, to a slimmed down version, to a shopping search engine, an e-commerce distribution platform, and finally on to a role as a thought leader in the new sector. "It's been fun!" Thanawat said.

Endnotes

1. CyberAgent Ventures Inc was established in 2006. Cyber Agent Inc, a company listed on the Tokyo Stock Exchange, was established in 1998 and is a Japanese Internet advertising agency with numerous subsidiaries, video game companies, and others, including CyberAgent Ventures: https://www.cyberagentventures.com/en/.
2. Susan Cunningham, "Priceza, PricePrice, Price-Panda - Who's Winning and Losing SE Asia's Price Comparison Races?" Forbes, 15 April 2015, https://www.forbes.com/sites/susancunningham/2015/04/15/priceza-priceprice-pricepanda-whos-winning-and-losing-se-asias-price-comparison-races/#645d886949d3.
3. Michael Tegos, "Thai price comparison startup gets series B to fuel growth beyond Southeast Asia", Tech In Asia, 28 September 2016, www.techinasia.com/priceza-series-b-funding.

Chapter 8

WONGNAI: IN THE MOOD
FOR MORE THAN FOOD

Wongnai, which means 'insider' in Thai, is a lifestyle portal that features over two hundred thousand restaurants, salons, spas, and other information across Thailand on its platform, together with details of each merchant and user reviews. Staying ahead of global and local competition is not easy in the disruptive world of start-ups and Wongnai is moving beyond its original focus and exploring other possibilities such as parenting sites and even pet services. CEO and co-founder, Yod Chinsupakul, is one of the business leaders behind the current crop of new generation businesses in Thailand, where he is now inspiring the next wave to find their passions and follow their dreams.

Its over two million registered users can search for what is top-rated in Bangkok, follow their friends, upload their food 'selfies' on to the site, and put quick write-ups about the places they have tried through Wongnai's location-based services on their mobile phone. Formerly a purely 'foodie' app, Wongnai has continued to innovate.

In 2015 it rolled out a major addition to its products, the e-voucher, which lets users avail discounts at merchant stores. It was the company's first move towards online-to-offline (O2O) services, a move that has built on its strong brand and solid user base and is a world away from the company's early days. Co-founder and

Wongnai CEO, Yod Chinsupakul, said it took 3G technology and smartphones to really open up the food app market in Thailand.

Back in 2010, he recalled, "I was using a Blackberry phone, which is a semi-smart phone. It wasn't as easy as it is now to install apps and here we were, trying to do location-based apps. I don't think we realised that the market wasn't ready. We were doing it because we thought it was a great idea".

Looking back, he said, "We were lucky that we didn't do any market research because if we did and found out that everyone was using Blackberry, like I was, we'd have thought that, hey, our idea is not going to work. The lesson learned here is that sometimes it's best if you just follow what you want to do. If you look too much into the market, maybe you don't get the chance to do it".

Market research is also sometimes flawed. "Looking back at the data, instead of looking forward at what the market needs, is a mistake we often make. Who could have predicted Starbucks?" To elaborate, there were innumerable marketing research studies done in the late 1980's and 1990's on the General Foods coffee data collected from retail checkout scanners. Large multi-market multi-site data sets allowed market researchers to develop advanced statistical models to predict consumer behaviours. All of that backward looking analysis certainly helped managers to fine tune their current strategies, but it totally missed the emergence of the differentiated flavour based coffee market. Looking at historical data rather than asking "What next? Or what if?" is a trap that often stifles innovation. But the team at Wongnai was always focused on what could be.

In its first year of operations, the site relied solely on desktop traffic, which is in sharp contrast to recent studies that show

Thai consumers are spending around five hours each day on their mobile phones. "Only a few people were using iPhones at that time", he said. This changed in 2012 when people switched from their old 'dumb' phones and Blackberry to the new 3G generation smart devices such as iPhones and Androids. When this switch took place (2012–2014), the number of Wongnai users jumped dramatically, from tens of thousands to over a million. "On hindsight, our timing was off by about a year".

There was not a lot of hope in the company's first two years. These were dark days: "We were burning through money, or not making money, because our users were not growing, and we were working insane hours". No users meant revenue was scarce. "I did approach some investors, but they weren't interested in investing in tech. Or maybe I wasn't well connected".

It was also a tough time to be thinking about raising money, let alone for a start-up. In 2010, there were no restaurant review websites in Thailand, the global financial crisis was afoot, and for Wongnai, there were a lot of costs, even though Yod had put in some family money.

Yod said he gave up trying to raise funds in the first two years and just focused on doing the business. "We didn't invest". He and fellow founders started to do outsourcing jobs such as programs, websites, and applications for other businesses just to keep afloat and continue to pursue the dream. "We used around fifty percent of our time — which is a lot — to keep the company running, but we were running at a loss".

Not knowing how to make money from the users was a key sticking point.

"We knew it was going to be advertising but it wouldn't be through banners because banners cannot scale that much. We recruited our first two sales people and then decided to look at what another firm, 'Recruit Group', was doing on the sales side".

Recruit's Hot Pepper site is considered second to top in terms of traffic, he said. "Their revenue is high because they have a very good sales management protocol and a sales force of more than 900 in Japan".

Yod increased the Bangkok sales force to five people, and then began to hire outside of the city. The sales force of thirty then proceeded to work with restaurants, local businesses, chains, and corporate clients, including brands and national advertisers. Sales staff attempted to match each of these groups by looking at their business models. "As we found initial success, we began to develop a marketing team, a data team, and then began to hire more developers".

Losses still dogged the company as it continued to add people. "We didn't have any money. But we were aggressive and we were ambitious", he said.

The Search for Capital

In 2012, negotiations for Pre-series A funding took place, with the first round of funding raised through Recruit Group from Japan. They remain a shareholder to this day.

Founded in 1960, the Recruit Group creates and provides platforms that connect companies and consumers with a wide range of services, including HR technology, recruitment advertisement, employment placement, staffing, housing and real estate, bridal, travel, dining, beauty, and others.[1]

Yod and the team visited Recruit three or four times. "What impressed me was their operational excellence, and that they moved fast, even though they're a big company". Their adaptability was another factor: they changed from a media company on the printing side to an online media company and now make money out of the internet business instead. How many companies can do that in the world? Not many!"

Recruit proved to be a natural fit and was able to ramp up the revenue side of the business. Yod was able to recoup all the money back that had been spent, and then used the rest to fund the company.

With the appearance of 3G, internet, smart phone penetration, and the shift of users to mobile, Wongnai grew from 30,000 to a million users in a couple of years. "Suddenly everything just exploded and we grew exponentially. The cash helped us grow".

They used all the money in one year and raised another round from the same investor in the next year. "We hit all the KPIs and they gave us another round of money. This meant we could grow the business for another two years". But this time they went through the money much slower as they had started to receive some revenue. "And we didn't spend as much".

Interestingly, he noted that even if they had the cash in 2010, the company wouldn't have grown because the market was not ready. But it was "super ready" in 2013, he says.

In 2016, another round of funding was raised from Intouch Group via Series B Funding through Intouch's venture capital arm, InVent,[2] an asset management company based in Thailand and engaged in telecommunications, media, IT, and digital content. The investment in Wongnai was the first ever series B investment in a Thai start-up made by a Thai venture capital firm and came with 38 million mobile subscribers as well as a strong network of local Small and Medium Enterprises (SMEs) in Thailand.

"The fresh cash was used to finance Wongnai's new online-to-offline (O2O) services and its expansion into other lifestyle verticals. It was another fortunate fit", Yod said, considering that eighty percent of the company's current traffic was coming from mobile.

Wongnai turned a corner and became profitable in 2017. "Sales got us there", he said. "We learned a lot from the Recruit Group. The single most important thing they taught us was sales".

The company now had more than two hundred and ten employees, mostly engineers and content staff.

Other Lessons

Other significant lessons learned prior to the launch of Wongnai came from a previous start-up where the hard years that he had put in with a Spanish friend in the United States eventually saw him return to Thailand in 2010.

The two friends created a social networking site along the lines of "Pinterest" while he was completing his MBA at the Anderson School of Management at the University of California, Los Angeles (UCLA). A combination of part-time job and a 'pet' project, it was not successful, he said. Not only was competition tight, there was no proper team, the site didn't launch properly, and they wound up with only a couple of hundred users.

More importantly, he said, there was no developer, which proved to be a major learning experience. The entrepreneurs, developing this business on a shoestring budget chose to outsource the development of the site. But, when they ran out of money, the developers quit and went on to other projects and the site ground to a halt. "By the time we had the money, they had other jobs. So they still couldn't do it. It was not flexible at all".

The lack of a development team proved to be their biggest obstacle. "As we are a tech start-up, the website — the program itself — is very important, because the site itself is the product. So when you outsource the core product to outsiders, then inevitably it will go wrong. In our case, we didn't have 'right software' for the market".

In general, outsourcing is a cheap and good idea, he said, until you have to have modifications made. "By then the developers have moved on, you are a small volume account, and they either don't want to work for you anymore or they have disbanded and are doing other things". Fortune 100 firms may have enough activity to keep outsourced vendors happy and interested in customizing or upgrading their past efforts. Unfortunately, start-ups do not garner the same commitment and attention from vendors. So continuity is a challenge.

Logistics and execution to one side, the formation of the actual team itself was central to success, he said. "In the end, I learned how to assemble a team, how to avoid the pitfalls, and how to design the product. All the basic stuff you need to do before acquiring customers".

Ideas Change, the Team Stays

Human resources are important when it comes to starting a business and are close to fifty percent of success, said Yod, especially for start-ups. "It's one of the most important things in the early stages. There's nothing in the way of assets in a start-up.

You just have the team. In our case we didn't have any funding at the time, not even a single line of code".

Ultimately, he concluded, a good team is actually more important than the idea. "A good team of developers is needed to make the product awesome. Because when the product sucks, then you can't market it".

In the case of Wongnai, his second start-up, Yod said he realised the need to assemble a team of good engineers. On a trip back to Thailand, he sought out his classmates from his Computer Engineering days at Chulalongkorn University and asked them to join the new company. "I went to high school with some of them, and elementary school in the case of another, so I knew they were good, their work ethic was sound, and they were the people I wanted to work with".

Engineers stick together, he said. And by the time he was in the final stages of his MBA in Los Angeles, the team was working together.

From 'Nom-nom' to Parenting and Pets

The team-based approach to ideation and problem solving — "Ideas change all the time, but the team stays the same" has been his preferred approach — can be seen in the far-sighted concept behind Wongnai.

Scenarios are created for people to enable them to view Wongnai as more of a lifestyle app that can connect them to a lot of good things, not just dining. "We didn't name ourselves Restaurant Review or Foodies. This was intentional. We wanted to give ourselves an opportunity to review many things. Even Yelp and TripAdvisor have different categories".

There were two 'light bulb' moments. The first was the reality that not a lot of websites focus only on one category, or that food is necessarily associated with everyone.

"We decided not to do food, but to concentrate on dining — eating outside. Even dining is not as broad as we think because there are only a handful of people with a certain disposable income who can dine or find a place to dine. At a certain income level, you won't see people eating outside that much, if at all, and in rural areas or in the suburbs, there won't even be a selection of restaurants". Therefore, if there are no choices available, "you won't need Wongnai".

The second was Wongnai's transformation into a lifestyle site in its fullest sense beginning with beauty products and services, which was started three years ago. It turned out to be very profitable, accounting for around twenty percent of revenue.

Reviewing salons, spas, and clinics might sound like a celebrity wish list, but in fact the number of users was not great, which meant Wongnai needed to grow both sides, the revenue side and users, as well as expand to even more categories in order to attract more people to use it more often.

Next up was cooking. Thailand lacked a good cooking portal. "When we started doing cooking videos, it was a little bit like 'Welcome to Tastemade,' a reference to the global community of food and travel lovers that offers quick recipes through to top-chef originals. We knew the demand was there, even just to find a good recipe for chicken rice".

Launched last year, advertisers loved it: there were lots of ingredients and kitchen appliances, and it was not location-based like the dining and beauty sites. "When you look at restaurants or spas, sites are really aimed at the large city. Most people in a small town know their local restaurants and the options do not change very often. Other than for the traveller, up-country restaurant information has a limited appeal". Ingredients and cooking appliances rapidly became a cash cow for the site because people are looking for things to do, not just things to eat, he explained. "Users flocked just to find out how to make chicken rice", he said.

"This year, the site will head to travel, a TripAdvisor for Thai people", a reference to the publicly-listed TripAdvisor, the American travel and restaurant website company that provides hotel and restaurant reviews, accommodation bookings, and other travel-related content.

"Pets and children might be next, with reviews of pet food and schools", he added.

Winner Takes All

Offering the market something that competitors cannot offer has proven to be another challenge in its own right. Recalling the early landscape in Thailand, Yod said Wongnai was faced with more than ten competitors, all of which were trying to do the same thing. "There was not much difference among us".

Competition included mega social foodie apps such as iPick, which belongs to Tencent.[3] Another was OpenRice.[4]

There were no appreciable differences in technology.

Wongnai relied on execution and knowledge of its consumers. OpenRice, he said, "had the technology and know-how, but they were not Thais. We were faster and attracted more users and more reviews".

Let's say, he continued, it was a little bit of — the winner takes all the market. "If this website has a lot of reviews, if I write a new review, why would I write a review on a smaller website? The more users, the more reviews I have, and the stronger I am".

Instagram, Facebook, and Google Maps

Over the last eighteen months, the competitive landscape has continued to face further disruption, where sites such as Wongnai — and other local sites, it must be added — need to evolve further to square off against Instagram, Facebook, and Google Maps, all of which have review facilities and can act as a significant disruptive force on the market.

"They're not food companies and they're not specific to food. It's partly because of this that we expanded to other things".

Facebook and Google might be the biggest websites in the world, but marketing is not their strength, he said. It doesn't have to be. "What attracts people to them is the product. Google's is its search engine. Like Facebook, it doesn't need to spend any advertising dollars, he explained.

But times change and DuckDuckGo, a search engine that emphasises protecting searchers' privacy and avoiding the filter bubble of personalised search results, is tilting at Google's supremacy as a search engine. Facebook has also started to lose favour among younger people and is showing fewer page results and more advertising, he said.

Searching to expand their reach and maintain their relevance has meant some of the early model social media behemoths have had to evolve. They might have started from search engines, but they are doing everything now. "Google Maps are on the upswing and offers restaurant reviews among simple directions, and hundreds of other products. Facebook has its e-Commerce". Line, a relatively new entrant but popular in Asia, has Line Man.[5]

Thailand is becoming an important market for many of them, he added, not necessarily the most important, but because they are used frequently. In Southeast Asia, Thailand is probably the second most important market behind Indonesia, he said.

They're not just coming in with their international version, they're trying to locally adapt with the idea of penetrating markets like Thailand, said Yod. "Google, for example, is focused heavily on the Thai market, Facebook not so much, Line is localised and very, very focused on the Thai market, while Instagram is not localised at all. It depends on who they are and how they view Thailand".

"This translates into the need for Wongnai to do more things to compete with Facebook and Google", he said, given the portal's aim is to connect people to everything that is good — dining, cooking, traveling, and beauty.

There are some overlaps. "Facebook has just launched the Facebook global app, and in the States, they are focused on finding food around you, which means they've entered our area. However, we are also in their space. If I ask people on the streets, how do you find a place to eat, things to do, they'll say Instagram. Or Facebook. Others might Google it and find a place on Google maps. Another five or so might use Instagram".

But, sometimes, he said, they will use Wongnai. "So we are in the same 'sentence' as these guys although we're smaller".

At this point, he said he and the team realised that no one is talking about OpenRice anymore. The temptation might have been to sit back and enjoy one less competitor, but it actually brought no respite from the competition for Wongnai.

In fact, Instagram is now the source of inspiration and food thrills for consumers. "To follow this person, go to this coffee shop. We [Wongnai] don't have that element, which means they are stealing time from us and other people", he observed.

"Broadly speaking, we need to recognise that our competitors are now the top five apps providers in Thailand", he said.

Mobility and Other Challenges

Interestingly the challenges faced by Wongnai are now emerging for the major credit card companies — for them, sustained and improved market penetration is essential for growth.

Like Wongnai, this is fine in the tier one cities such as the Bangkok's, Jakarta's or Singapore's of the world, but it's problematic in rural markets or tier three markets where there are no transactions, while a small town with one or two food outlets means a food review or delivery service would not prove to be as meaningful.

Another similarity is the use of influencers. But rather than work with celebrities, Yod said he preferred the 'wisdom of the crowd.' "Sometimes they are our market channels and we pay them to promote our apps. However, we believe more in our visiting crowd than the expert. Our platform is made for the crowd — the wisdom of the crowd — for normal people. Or even for the wannabes, rather than the celebrities. I find celebrity influencers really hard to control", he said. "People don't put a great deal of stock in their credibility these days. That's been the findings all across these websites".

A key issue for both sectors, which are huge given their reach into lifestyle, is therefore how to move beyond tier one and tier two cities and further.

Wongnai quickly recognised that restaurant reviews were only good in the major metro areas where restaurants and food outlets come and go. "Consumers are unlikely to know all of them", he said. But that's not the case in small towns where the restaurants are known and a review has little value, except for a traveller. The decision to broaden its scope, seek partnerships, and move into lifestyle has kept the company fresh and growing, said Yod.

"Just because we started from food, it doesn't mean we have to do food. We are actually an internet company of Thai people, so we want to connect Thai people to all the good stuff".

Moveable Feasts

"When people are in the mood for food, they don't have to go out for it, it comes to them", Yod said of the partnership with Line. The decision to offer the delivery service was both pragmatic and anticipatory to ensure the company's continuing survival: food delivery services meet a changing consumer lifestyle.

Opportunities have continued to open. Wongnai recently joined Lalamove, another on-demand logistics company in Asia.[6] Interestingly, Lalamove is currently partnering with IKEA in Singapore, Sony Pictures Bangkok, and Lazada Singapore, a mind-boggling — even Byzantine — network with interesting prospects for all concerned.

Not only are things well and truly on the move in the foodie apps realm, with food delivery remaining a hot space, there are now lots of people in that space. In time they will certainly want to grow beyond their core as well. To thrive and grow in that space requires Olympic class agility.

But at its core, Wongnai's strength is its team. Harnessing some of the sharpest young tech minds and putting them to the task of creating "something cool for Thai people" has produced a magic that is state of the art. A firm that is ready for the next battle against some of the world's giants.

Endnotes

1. Recruit Holdings, https://recruit-holdings.com/.
2. Judith Balea, "Thai startup Wongnai scores B funding for big O2O push", Tech In Asia, 27 April 2016, https://www.techinasia.com/wongnai-series-b-invent.
3. Andre Chan, "Introducing IPick—The New Social Foodie App for All Your Om Nom Nom Needs", mobile88.com, 25 April 2016, http://www.mobile88.com/news/feature/ipick-new-social-foodie-app-for-all-your-om-nom-nom-needs/.
4. OpenRice is owned by JDB Holdings, the owner and operator of online media portals and networks with services such as jobs, services, restaurants, maps, clothing, cars, beauty products, and flower delivery services: https://www.investing.businessweek.wallst.com/research.
5. Line Man is Line's first foray into local, on-demand services. Refer Steven Millward, "Line launches spin-off app to deliver stuff to your

doorstep", Tech In Asia, 16 May 2016, https://www.techinasia.com/line-launches-line-man.

6. Catherine Shu, "On demand logistics startup Lalamove scores $10m to fuel its China Expansion", Tech Crunch.Com, 9 September 2015, https://techcrunch.com/2015/09/09/on-demand-logistics-startup-lalamove-scores-10m-to-fuel-its-china-expansion/.

Chapter 9

AT VANTAGE MARKETING RESEARCH: TAKING ON THE GLOBAL RESEARCH GOLIATHS

Sometimes the journey is clear but the destination only takes shape after the trip begins. Suttipan Sutas Na Ayuthaya (Mhom), the managing partner at At Vantage Co. Ltd., a Thai market research agency, has had a rather straightforward and simple corporate agenda: "To provide our clients with the best information possible to make good business decisions". Executing that plan hasn't always been so straightforward. He and his co-founders had noticed that the profession was increasingly unable to deliver on its true potential to the rapidly evolving Thai consumer landscape. Dominated by the large multinational research houses with their slick presentations and global reputations, Thai firms tended to receive standardised cookie-cutter reports that did very little to assist local firms in meeting emerging market challenges. For that matter, the multinational firms that were attempting to enter the Thai market also struggled to gain accurate and comprehensive insights. The opportunity was there as it was time for a change.

Distinguishing itself by the presentation style and the intellectual problem-solving skills of its founder, At Vantage is today a major force in the Thailand market research industry. By bringing business analysts, enhanced software, and data science under one roof, this local David has been able to take on the four global research Goliaths. As it enters its second decade of serving its clients' need for better insights, At Vantage is poised for global expansion.

The Early Days

To understand the journey of At Vantage, one needs to understand its founder's path. The route chosen was despite, or in spite of, two major crises: the 1997 financial crisis and the 9/11 bombing of the World Trade Center in New York in 2001.

"I was in the United States when the financial crisis hit in Thailand. I was not from a wealthy family and the crisis devastated my father's business. There was simply no money for me to go to school in the States, in fact there really was not enough money for me to continue my studies when I came back to Thailand. I needed to work if I was going to continue studying, and so I began to look at taking up a job. One of my friends came to me and said, 'My uncle is a director at EGV (a cinema chain which was a joint venture between an Austrian company and a Hong Kong firm) and he needs some market research done. I gave him your name.' And so I started off".

Mhom began the project with his friend's uncle, thinking he would quietly report the findings to the uncle. This was his first solo market research project and it was more than enough to pay for his tuition and fees. But, at the tender age of 22, he found himself presenting in front of the suits in a boardroom in Bangkok. Still in his final year of undergraduate studies, he was facing the company's board of directors and senior management, which included a number of marketing professionals.

It was "daunting (he recalls). I was freaking out — literally. But I kept my cool. I thought it kind of went okay, because before the meeting people called me Suttipan, but by the end of the meeting they were all calling me 'Mhom' — my nickname. I took that as an indication that the presentation was probably okay".

It turned out it was more than okay! EGV management later offered him a job. Not just any job, they wanted him to set up their entire marketing research department. He recalls: "I didn't know I was interviewing for a job, but that is how I got my first job, and it was as the manager of the New Investment Department, which was essentially an in-house market research department".

Over the next several years, Mhom learned a lot about how to organize, manage, conduct, and present the results of market research projects. His passion for market research continued to grow.

Mhom wanted to pursue his Masters' degree. But, after living on the financial edge as a student, his only thoughts about the Masters were whether he could "make money off this. It is a very different situation to when your parents are paying", he recalled.

He had accumulated some savings and decided to attend the Kelley School of Business, at Indiana University. Kelley was well known for teaching quantitative decision-making and market research skills, according to Mhom. However, when a plane hit the World Trade Center, "My plans changed".

His former professor, Randall Shannon suggested him to join Thammasat's Masters in Marketing (MIM) program, where Professor James Nelson was teaching conjoint analysis, a hot topic in the late 1990s. "I didn't care about any other subject", he said. "I just wanted to learn conjoint analysis so that I could use it to make money. I really saw this as a great tool to help managers gain insights into the trade-off between features".

Conjoint (also referred to as trade-off analysis) is a survey-based statistical technique that is often employed in designing new products and services. Broadly speaking, respondents share with you the products they prefer as different levels of attributes are varied. For instance, you might ask what people would like in a computer, and find they want it to be fast, cheap, and lightweight. That would seem obvious. However, the real questions in designing often centres around — what would they prioritise or what are they willing to trade off? Would they rather have a lower price in exchange for a greater weight or a slower speed? How much more would they pay for maximum speed, or for the lowest weight? By comparing their trade-off decisions, you can understand the customer's preference and ranking for each variable. These holistic trade-offs allow you to view the prioritisation when a combination of features, functions, or design elements are present.

Mhom wound up entering the MIM program. Emboldened with his new conjoint analysis skills, he "did all kinds of jobs", graduated, and, importantly, remained open to learning.

Still at EGV, Mhom became restless and soon struck out on his own. However, after his parents' struggles into business ownership, Mhom was not very keen to start a firm and initially began by doing freelance work. But when people found out he was no longer with EGV, they started to call with research projects. Times were personally challenging. He recounts: "I either had to continue to make money as a freelancer where, for the first time in my life, I had one million Thai Baht in my bank account, or strike out on my own. I truly believed that marketing research could be more than what was being offered by the local 'cookie cutter' firms, which don't reflect the true potential of market research".

When a team member from his EGV days, Voravimol, asked him if he wanted to start a marketing research firm, Mhom said "yes" over an instant messenger (IM) chat. With that message, the founding team of Mhom, Randall Shannon, and Voravimol began At Vantage Marketing Research.

The Early Days: Moving Out of the Corporate Space

Mhom believed a great market opportunity existed in Thailand's growing economy and rapidly evolving consumer markets. Having conducted in-house market research and purchased the services of the "Big Four", he had developed a distaste for the way market research was sold and conducted in Thailand. He was convinced that there was a place for At Vantage; although he admitted that he didn't really understand the ins and outs of owning a company.

He found cheap office space in Bangkok's Royal City Avenue district, better known as RCA, right in the heart of the city's clubbing and nightlife zone. The company grew and three years later, it moved to Asoke Towers, a larger building that could house his growing staff of nearly 40.

From the early days, Mhom's marketing approach was simply to call on the clients that were large and mature enough to appreciate high-quality market research. "I wanted to call on the firms that were sophisticated enough to use outside vendors, and their price point was high enough to provide us with the margins we needed to provide quality. It was a chicken and egg thing. I needed these types of clients to sell my services to others. The reason being that if I had never gone to them before, they would think 'why would I trust a local?' They would just go with an international firm. But if I could get to the ones who were already using the international firms, then there would be a chance, and they could see the quality of what I was doing and that it could meet their requirements". The strategy worked.

He grew the company by offering cutting edge solutions with exceptional technical qualities. He explained, "Working at At Vantage, we routinely applied more statistics than a typical big firm might be willing to provide. I literally invested in analysis".

A modern approach to reports and presentations was also used to position the company. Mhom made the decision to move right away to visual and graphics-driven reports. This was a distinct departure from the prevailing text-heavy reports of the time, and enabled At Vantage to differentiate itself from the Big Four. "I wanted everything to stand out, use fancy graphics, models, building blocks, clean, clear messaging, those kinds of things". Where the Big Four sold their ideas on templates, At Vantage customised.

The approach was also in the client's interests: "They need visuals if they are to build consensus and offer insights to their audiences and stakeholders. Audiences don't understand numbers and calculations, but they do sit up and take notice when it comes to pie charts and trend lines. We needed to provide dashboards, not calculations".

Developing New Competencies

From their earliest days, the team at At Vantage had never hesitated to take on stretch projects that would help them develop new skills. The firm's first large account was AP Honda, the largest operation of Honda Motorcycle worldwide. The Honda experience, in particular, provided important insights. The client wanted to understand service quality, but was unable to make much use of the research because it was all mail-based at the time. Receiving data that was often out of date and from a distant time-period made it hard to know what activities were gaining traction in the marketplace, as they were not sure what time periods the customers were evaluating (that is, the time response rate could not be controlled). From a research perspective, a manager wouldn't know where to start to fix the problems in the market.

"This was also the era when even one megabyte of speed was not available", Mhom playfully recalled as he recounted the difficulty of creating and turning around thirty-eight unique reports for thirty-eight Honda outlets within a very tight time frame. Not only was it difficult to gather the response rates to questionnaires, it was also difficult to attribute the questionnaires to the right dealerships. However, the questionnaires were not the hard part. Reports had to be sufficiently detailed or simple as the case may be to meet the expectations of the sales person as well as the owner of the outlet in order for them to see how to improve their store.

Honda was the first time At Vantage outsourced its IT services. Mhom's team had the ideas but could not progress further and develop an information system to build a robust data capture platform without the support of an IT firm. So he began to go beyond the mail survey data collection techniques and aggregation of a paper and pencil survey, to online completion of surveys. This enabled At Vantage to collect much larger quantities of data that were better time sequenced and easier to attribute to specific stores. "The future of market research, as I saw it, was certainly beginning to change. Suddenly we began to capture, look at, and analyse much larger data sets. In the old days we would try to get two or three respondents from each of the 38 stores every month, and that was a challenge! Now we were literally able to analyse thousands of records every day at every store for some of our large retail clients".

Mhom was at home in this sort of environment as the firm and the teams were learning how to perform more complex work and be of greater service to their clients. Professionally, he was fulfilled with the firm's evolving capabilities. From the earliest days of the organisation, he had said, "I want to be the production guy. I will take care of executing the market research work, and let others run the business and finances". The early years of At Vantage were characterised by steady growth as it developed an enviable customer list of the top consumer packaged goods, automotive, banking, airlines, and retail firms in Thailand. Revenues kept growing as these clients came aboard. But much to the chagrin of the partners, the bottom line was stuck. Market research at the time was a business that offered little opportunity for scale. This point was especially true if you were going to customise your work to client needs.

The Revenue Versus Costs Conundrum

Like other professional service firms, Mhom found that while the company revenue might be able to grow sharply, it was hard to maintain and predict as client needs were not always constant. This was a risky matter for firms that obtained more bottom line through sheer sales growth rather than by higher margins or lower costs. Managing even larger accounts becomes riskier as you hire people in anticipation of sales growth, but then, as Mhom said, the eternal question was, "What if they [clients] don't continue?"

What was needed, he said, was for revenue to grow faster than costs, or costs to go up slower than the revenue. In the case of manufacturing firms, he understood that a large market share could lead to higher profitability because manufacturing was scalable and pushing more volume through your factory or machines did not greatly increase the cost of using those fixed assets. But service firms do not always scale up like that, he pointed out. "You begin to find when you start hiring people that it's not hard to find two good market research people. But when you have to hire twenty, it is nearly impossible. Suddenly you're moving down the quality pool a bit".

Similarly, outsourcing was not a solution. "Just to change a button needs a conversation and as they don't own the coding, small modifications can't be done without the other firm coming in. If you don't have a solid relationship with the firm you outsource to, then they're on to other projects, so you have to be a regular customer. It's difficult to manage an outsourced software development group. You become quite vulnerable".

Ultimately, the company's financial reports were a wake-up call and he was forced to look at smarter ways of doing things, moving out from under his production silo. "In the early days, I was just making sure that I could pay for what's going on. One day my wife, Anya, the finance person in our family, forced me to give her the P&L statement. After she read it, she yelled at me and asked why I hadn't looked at it. Well... I said, I'm just a production guy".

She was blunt. "Are you enjoying the projects or are you building your future?" It made me sit up and think, he said. "I really had to face the truth and look at the numbers. Once I started to think about my future responsibilities, I started to look at the platforms".

In the end, his 'pathway to profitability' came in the form of platform creation rather than continuing to take jobs on a one-by-one basis.

Bringing All Platforms Under One Roof

Step 1: The Rise of Analytics

Mhom recalled, "In the early days, local research firms were more focused on the cranking out of data and less on intelligence. Their process was actually quite disjointed and conducted in a serial manner. The solicitation was its own process. The Big Four had researchers going out to clients, getting briefed, coming back with the brief, designing a research proposal, and going back to the client. If the client agreed with the proposal, the work would begin. When it came time to do the work, it was again a step-by-step process. After a questionnaire was constructed, it was passed to the field team, and after completion, it would find its way to the data processing team. Tabulations would be sent to the researcher, and the analysis sent on to a chart-producing team. The researcher then had to read the chart and fine-tune or restart the analysis. That's how the Big Four worked. When I looked at this work structure, I knew At Vantage had to be different at the organisational level".

Mhom decided to introduce a new division into the organisation. Known as Client Services, the field was non-existent in the marketing research industry at that time. At Vantage was the only firm to send a client service team to meet with the client. Most of the team were BBA and MBA graduates with very average marketing research knowledge. But they did understand the problems of marketing and promotion. Some of them also came from the client side, which meant they spoke the language of the customer and were therefore able to understand the business needs of the customer. Their business insights were then translated for the marketing research group.

This Client Services department enabled At Vantage to better serve its client needs. In the emerging era of 'Big Data', many managers incorrectly assumed that large amounts of data can overcome problems in the research question. Or more simply, that if there is more data, any question can be answered. This was not true, as managers were finding that gaining meaningful insights was not about how much data was collected, but about starting with an understanding of the questions that needed to be answered and the information required to make decisions. For routine and well-understood problems, IT professionals and data-scientists were fully capable of collecting the information and analysing it — but when the problems were novel and not completely understood, it was more about structuring the research hypotheses to ask for the right data.

Step 2: Automation and the Ability to Scale

Compared to the old ways of carrying out market research, where automation was non-existent and when the number of bodies needed to do each project was relatively the same, e.g., one hundred hours to do one hundred field interviews, the benefits of the new approach were obvious. Mhom shook his head: "Nowadays, using online surveys, we need zero hours of field researchers to collect one hundred surveys. All we really need is someone to programme an electronic mailer. From a cost standpoint, automating in the software driven online world was a no-brainer".

Research panels were another area where scale and flexibility could be improved. "Panels were not used on the scale they are today", he said, of the market research panels in which a group of recruited survey respondents agree to take part in surveys and/or other market research, and extensive information about themselves and their households was gathered and used for appropriate sample selection immediately. "You no longer need to go out and find people. They're always available and you can reach them, even four hundred people if you need, whenever you want, at the click of a button".

Of the large panel firms at the time, none were research firms. He said, "The majority were marketing firms that sold access to their panels".

"This has squeezed the industry at one end, although the call of comprehensive analytics beckons at the other. Before the world woke up with the term 'Big Data', most of a company's marketing decisions would be through either Enterprise Resource Planning (ERP) analysis or through internal marketing research".

Nowadays, he said, marketing departments have a huge amount of analytics and information available to them 24/7, and at their fingertips. There is no longer any need to go out and ask small groups of consumers for their opinions.

Step 3: Digitalisation

The wake-up call saw Mhom move At Vantage to a firm focused on creating value in the processes that it used. He began to develop his own software rather than outsourcing, and started to consider owning a software development unit.

It was not something he had imagined when he started the company. "My main drive for starting software development was to bridge the relationship between revenue and cost". In fact, the decision meant At Vantage was now in a unique position in that it provided clients with a one-stop shop, where they no longer had to rely on third parties or software consulting firms. Mhom's decision had nothing to do with the digitalisation of the world at all, he said, it was about providing a new revenue structure to the firm, and hence driven by financial needs. It was also about meeting the customers' needs. They did not want to go to three or four firms to get their market intelligence; they needed it under one roof.

As clients began to ask for such customisation, Mhom was recognising the power of analytics, which was in the process of revolutionising the market research business.

It was at this point, armed with technology and software, he struck out and transformed the company from a 'marketing research firm', where research was just one of the services the company provided, to a full-fledged 'marketing intelligence firm'.

At Vantage was sufficiently nimble to seize the moment and move out of the slog of conducting market research one step at a time. Everything is now under the one roof, he said. "My researcher has full access to my software features, understands how it works, and if we want to improve the algorithm, we have in-house data scientists". Modifications can also be done in-house, which means clients don't have to mix and match three or four different vendors".

"I think it's lucky that I was able to stay away from traditional market research, before the ship sank completely. Right now, the industry is almost under water".

Five Easy Pieces: Advice to a Younger Self

As his twentieth year in market research approached, Mhom was in some ways a different person, yet in other ways he was the same. The skills he had developed had changed him, and running a business that made him responsible for the livelihoods of other people had changed his views on business. But, his passion for market research in figuring out that new insight that comes from bringing a problem-solving mindset to an area rich with data has never wavered. This would have been an unrequited love though, if it were not for his ongoing quest for knowledge, a state of mind that had seen him embrace and expand the modern research continuum as it travelled from paper-based, to non-paper based, electronic data collection.

As At Vantage begins to look at new technologies and new international markets, it seemed an appropriate time to review the journey, and Mhom reflected on the five key insights that began to emerge from his journey:

1. Passion: Start with passion. Do something you love doing. When you do something that you are passionate about, it is much easier to put in the effort to improve and to expand. Few businesses have all the pieces you need for success. You will have to make changes and adaptations to your strategy and your organisation. It is much easier to take on these challenges when you have a passion for your work.

2. Never set simple wealth as the objective of your business: Do not start with opportunity as you may be discouraged by the initial projections. Do not start with how big the market is today. If you can imagine what it could be tomorrow, you can grow a small market into a vibrant market for the future.

3. Do not just study hard, but continue to study so you can pursue your passion: Too often study is undertaken without a goal in sight. Even as a student, Mhom was clear that whatever courses he would take was with the idea to become a better market researcher. The journey often goes much swifter when you know where you are going.

4. You cannot be afraid to change: During the journey of At Vantage, there have been many changes in focus, operational

activities, technologies, and even the manner in which clients are engaged. To succeed, you have to be nimble, flexible, and open to change.

5. Believe in your ability even when it's a case of local David vs. global Goliaths: Mhom reflects, "Did I bother about it, or stop and think about this for a second? No. I believed in my ability to communicate and deliver the values".

Looking back on the ride and the experience, like Harley riders, Mhom has relished the speed and the wound-up rumble of the motor. "I'm in marketing intelligence. I never feel like I'm working. I enjoy it. It's a challenge. I'm having fun. But I'm not so sure whether or not my staff will have the same fun I've had over the years!"

Chapter 10

ALTO COFFEE: BREWING THE PREMIUM COFFEE PROPOSITION

At Alto Coffee, a retail and wholesale coffee business based in Bangkok, the smell of a successful coffee recipe is certainly in the air. But, the path to today's growing enterprise did not come without a few pivots. Patthrapon Ruangsuteerakit ("Tae"), owner and business development manager of Alto Coffee, explains that if you are driven by numbers or quantity, and not quality, it may not matter now, but it will matter three to five years down the road — and that is important, because they plan to be there for the long run.

Owner and operator of four coffee shops in Bangkok and a supplier of specialty grade roasted coffee beans to numerous Food and Beverage (F&B) outlets around Bangkok and central Thailand, Tae's introduction to coffee began during his undergraduate days in the US. After graduating in 2005, he returned to Bangkok and set up a business to sell premium grade pasteurised soy milk. In 2007, as sales did not take off as planned, the soy milk business was wound down and Tae started a café business in the Central Business District in Bangkok to preserve jobs for some of his staff from the soy milk business. Three cafes, opened six months apart, were established to sell the same coffee at different price points, and served as an experimental ground for Tae to understand what consumers liked in their coffee. He soon decided to also move into coffee roasting and the wholesale side of the business.

In 2012, Tae closed down the three cafes after his initial experiment, and proceeded to open Alto Coffee, an outlet that would sell premium coffee. The Alto Coffee store was opened as a 'boutique café' — it was a café, sold coffee beans, and sold coffee-making equipment too. Not only was the store run by well-trained staff, Tae also made sure that he sourced the best quality coffee beans; he even handled the roasting and blending process himself. Tae's goal was to sell premium quality coffee, and he wanted to gain the interest of his customers in the product by educating them about coffee through various touch points and constant communication.

In early 2012, Tae set up a roasting facility and a few months later, in May 2012, he established the first store at Megabangna — a shopping mall in Bangkok. In the first year of business in 2012, revenue was around US$125,000 with a 10 percent contribution from wholesale.

By October 2017, Tae had opened the fourth Alto store in Bangkok, and his ambitions were very high — but he also wanted to make the right decisions to ensure that his business would succeed.

Food and Beverage in Thailand

Due to increasing urbanisation and a higher percentage of women entering the workforce (46% of the workforce in 2010), more people were eating out, and the food-service industry in Thailand, valued at US$23 billion in 2010, was slated to grow at a compound annual growth rate of 2% till 2015.

Specialist chain coffee shops were slated to grow the fastest in the café and bar sector, with a growth rate of 9% in 2010. In 2010,

Starbucks was by far the leader amongst the top ten café chains in Thailand with a 45% market share, followed by Black Canyon coffee with 13% market share.

Totalling about 1,200 outlets throughout Thailand, café chains such as Starbucks and Coffee World were located mostly in shopping malls and office buildings, whilst others such as Café Amazon and Caffe D'Oro were found at petrol kiosks. Although competition between local and international coffee chains was strong, there were plans by many of the players to expand in the market, with some coffee chains even going into the restaurant business.

Getting into the Coffee Business

Tae spent his childhood in Bangkok, but attended school in Singapore for nine years, before doing his undergraduate degree in food science at Pennsylvania State University in the U.S. in 2001. Although his family business was in real estate, his parents were open-minded and supportive of Tae's desire to study food science as a first degree, before pursuing a more business-related degree of Masters in Marketing later on in Bangkok. During Tae's stay in the U.S., he did a six-month internship working in an ice cream factory in upstate New York, and another six months working as a supervisor at a coffee chain in Washington D.C., and that was when he started to learn about coffee making. After graduating in 2005, Tae moved home to Bangkok in 2006.

Tae saw an opportunity to bring soy milk into the Thai market. In the U.S., there were good quality alternatives to milk for the lactose intolerant, such as the milk brand 'Silk', but there was only one brand of pasteurised soy milk in the Thai market at that time and it was not considered to be of very good quality. In 2007, together with his brother who had studied industrial engineering, Tae started up his first business to manufacture premium grade pasteurised soy milk in Thailand. While Tae was in charge of research and development, his brother was responsible for setting up the machinery for soy milk production and streamlining operations.

By September 2009, the company was bringing in monthly revenues of around US$30,000; 85% of the revenue went to cover raw materials and operating costs. The majority of sales were from limited modern trade stores, health food stores, hospitals, and Japanese restaurant chains. Sales growth was mainly by acquisition of new outlets and clients, and not by organic growth, as there was insufficient interest for the product in the Thai market. It was found that customers were not willing to pay more, as they did not see soy milk as a premium product and Tae's product did not appear sufficiently differentiated from the competitors. Additionally, the pasteurised soy milk had to be delivered and stored in cold storage at all times with only two weeks' shelf life. This put a limitation to expanding and exploring new distribution channels. In the end, the brothers decided to exit the business at a loss, and sold off whatever capital assets they could, as many of the machinery parts were specific to soy bean milk manufacture and could not be sold.

The First Three Coffee Outlets

The next business idea came about toward the end of 2009. The soy milk venture was closing down, and Tae wanted to keep as many as possible of his 20 staff employed in that venture by moving them to a new business. Learning from his previous failure, Tae had two key objectives. One, the new business must be a product that already had existing consumers in a growing market. Two, Tae preferred that the new business be cash-based, and he have control over his own product rather than depending on the 'modern trade' channels to look out for his interests. Tae decided to open up cafes as he had some familiarity with the coffee business from his student days. His focus was on opening outlets in the Central Business District of Bangkok, as he predicted a high volume of coffee consumption in the office areas.

Tae opened his first café in 2009, and the second and third café followed within six months of each other. He recalled, "I needed to get the new business started as soon as possible, and I was fortunate to be able to take a loan from my family, which I promised to pay back with interest".

The same cup of coffee was sold at different price points across the three cafes, ranging from US$1.30 to US$2.10. Tae used the three outlets as a base for market research to experiment and gain insights on the new business — varying the menu names, cup size, sales promotion, and colour of packaging to give the coffee shops a different look and feel. At these price points, he believed it did not make sense to spend any money on marketing. He observed, "Customers in this segment were price sensitive, but many were also sceptical that good quality coffee could be sold at US$1.60 when Starbucks coffee was retailing at US$3.50".

Tae also realised that he could only achieve the quality of coffee he wanted if he roasted his own coffee beans. That was when he decided to move into coffee roasting and planned to sell his coffee wholesale. At the same time, he had been receiving feedback from customers that because his coffee outlets were in the Central Business District, they were location-bound — it was difficult for customers to enjoy his coffee on the weekend or elsewhere. That prompted Tae's second idea to bring coffee into the homes of the consumers by selling roasted coffee beans and brewing equipment.

Alto Coffee

Tae and his brother spent a year planning for a new coffee concept store that would replace the three outlets that they had opened, and help them promote both retail and wholesale coffee. This time, Tae was managing the marketing and operations aspects of the business, while his brother handled finances and cost management. Alto Coffee was opened in May 2012 at Megabangna, one of the largest malls in Southeast Asia. It was important that Alto's location had high visibility, and the mall's location made it a good catchment area for traffic from two major routes into and out of Bangkok. It was also near Bangkok's main airport. The mall's tenants included many established brands and restaurants that were popular with Thai consumers (such as the Swedish furniture designer IKEA), and on a given weekend, it would be visited by an estimated 100,000 people. There were also many residential areas springing up in the surrounding area and young families were moving in. Because Alto wanted to go into the wholesale business as well, it was not a priority for them to open in a downtown location, where the rental costs would be significantly higher.

Décor and Menu

Tae decided on the name 'Alto' as it was short and easy to remember, and it meant "high" in Italian, referring to the Italian-styled espresso coffees and the high quality coffees sourced from high altitude (coffee grown at higher altitudes is considered to be more rich and flavourful than coffee grown at lower altitudes as the cooler temperatures enable coffee beans to grow more slowly). The Alto Coffee space was divided into a showroom for coffee beans and coffee equipment, a coffee bar, and seating areas. Tae went to great effort to re-design the store to optimise it for retail profits. In contrast to many cafes where customers are allowed to spend a long time sitting, studying, or working, the electrical outlets from the walls were removed to encourage higher customer turnover. This was a way to persuade the customers who just wanted a place to work to move elsewhere, making room for coffee lovers to come in for a short break and be on their way. He also reduced the number of seats in the café, dedicating more space to the coffee equipment displays and products with higher price compared to a coffee drink. These changes helped to further increase retail revenues. Tae elaborated, "This change was effective and also possible to implement as the café was located in a shopping mall, where customers could grab their coffees and be on their way to shop and hang out at the mall".

Menu pricing was kept simple, with one price for hot and cold coffees, which made it easy for staff to communicate with customers. The price point of US$3.40–$4.50 for a specialty coffee drink was based on feedback given by customers at Tae's earlier stores, as well as the market value at that time. Customers were becoming more educated and aware of what they were consuming, with a willingness to spend more — if the quality and taste met their expectations. The prices at Alto Coffee were 10–15% lower compared to those in the global coffee chains. In addition to specialty coffees, Alto Coffee also sold various teas, chocolate, fusion drinks, and bakery products to reach out to wider target groups.

A Premium Coffee Offering

As a child, Tae had been inculcated with a family value to "do something well, else not do it at all". He used this philosophy to uphold his dedication to serve high quality products to his customers. Alto used 100% specialty grade Arabica coffee beans from various coffee farms and estates from all over the world, including locally from the northern part of Thailand. Arabica bean was of a higher grade compared to the other commonly grown coffee beans like Robusta, as it had better aroma, sweetness, and smoother taste compared to Robusta which was more bitter and less flavourful. He also experimented with various roasting techniques to develop different taste profiles to suit different target consumers. For example, the coffee beans used to make hot coffee drinks were a medium-roast blend from Africa and South America, as that showcased their aroma and flavours, while an iced coffee drink would use a darker roast from Central America and Asia as it had a richer and stronger aftertaste to balance out the melting ice. Tae also procured better coffee-making equipment for his shop, paying up to double the price of a basic coffee machine to achieve the taste of what he called 'good coffee'. In his words, "Quality coffee is aromatic, tastes sweet and clean, with minimal bitterness in the mouth. Fresh roasted coffee always smells and tastes better".

Due to Tae's dedication to producing premium coffee, Alto's costs had increased by 20% in its first year of opening, but Tae felt that it was worth it. He added, "We could easily have taken funding and opened ten branches, but I was not going to compromise on the quality. When we can tell the difference, it doesn't matter if the customers can't".

Tae and his staff had to often convince his customers to change their perception of the taste of Alto's coffee (as it was frequently compared to Starbucks), and was something of an acquired taste. He observed, "Now people keep coming back [for Alto coffee] because they cannot find this unique taste elsewhere. People are starting to cultivate a taste for it, like wine. That's why we are so obsessed about quality". Alto was open seven days a week, till as late as 9 pm, as Tae wanted to have his coffee available right through the long opening hours of the shopping mall.

Staff in the retail outlet had to not only prepare coffee, but also be able to engage customers in a knowledgeable conversation about the various types of coffee sold in the shop. The training process for any new staff was thorough — they were required to attend a month-long in-house training program before they were allowed to make coffee for the customers. The training covered aspects ranging from coffee knowledge, to learning how to make different types of coffees, to food hygiene and customer service.

Tae would sometimes sit in a corner of the café and quietly observe his staff, noting how they interacted with customers and handled queries, and occasionally gave them feedback on how to improve their skillsets. Not all staff aspired to that level of service and attention to detail, but those who had stayed with Alto were well-compensated compared to the industry average.

Going Up the Supply Chain

Behind the storefront, Tae was also busy making sure all the conditions were right for him to make his premium coffee — and the process began at the farm. Tae made several trips every year to Chiang Mai and Chiang Rai (northern part of Thailand) to visit coffee farms, to learn from the farmers, and provide them with updated information about new studies and methods that were being done around the world. From understanding the plant species, choosing the farms with favourable growing conditions, to cleaning and processing the beans after harvest, building a relationship with the farmers and processors was very important. Tae chose to work with only a few reliable and ethical suppliers who met the standards and specifications of Alto. Giving back to the farm community and improving the standard of living of the farmers was just as important, and that was the driving reason behind Alto's willingness to buy coffee beans at 25–30% above market price from the farmers.

Alto sold several blended coffees and seasonal single-origin coffees. Besides sourcing from Thailand, Tae also worked with leading coffee traders to import coffee beans from well-known coffee estates all over the world, such as Guatemala, Colombia, and Kenya, which he would blend with local beans to create the unique tastes. Thai coffee beans were reserved and bought once a year during harvest season as per market practice, and the other beans were imported quarterly. Coffee would be blended every week to create a taste that was the most balanced for that particular batch of beans.

The Retail Business

By October 2013, Alto had been open for one and a half years and was Tae's only retail store. One year later, another store and Training Room was opened at Ploenchit Center, an office tower in Bangkok. In March 2016, a third store was set up at Suanplern Market, a community mall. In October 2017, a fourth store was established at the Central World shopping mall.

When Alto first started operations, 90% of revenues had come from retail and 10% from wholesale; as of 2018, it stood at 75% retail and 25% wholesale. Tae said, "I want to build a brand for retail, and create a market for wholesale". He further explained, "The wholesale numbers are actually difficult to grow in proportion, because with each new store opening, the retail sales will spike up and make the wholesale numbers even smaller by comparison".

Tae wanted the store to be not so much a sit-down place for the retail customers, but rather to create an experience for both the retail and wholesale customers. To achieve this, the environment in Alto Coffee was designed to pique the interest of anyone who walked into the store. A section of every store with high visibility was dedicated to retail display for coffee beans and equipment, to emphasise the brand's positioning as a coffee roaster and supplier.

For first-time customers, Alto had a feel and look like "a chain store from overseas". Thai consumers were the number one user of Facebook outside of the US, and Tae designed the shop and the drinks to create maximum photo opportunities when customers entered the shop. Tae said, "Nothing is placed here [in the shop] by chance. We want it exactly there for a reason". For example, at the counter where customers waited to collect their coffee, Tae had placed a set of unique cold drip coffee equipment to intrigue coffee lovers. They would then ask questions so that the staff could engage them.

Alto's target market for retail was, in Tae's words, "People who were unpretentious, didn't have to dress up to enjoy a good café experience, and were casual and comfortable". As opposed to Starbucks' dark interiors, Alto Coffee had bright lighting. Tae wanted to attract 'honest and sophisticated people' who understood Alto's philosophy, and also the 25-and-above age group who would be willing to spend on premium coffee, when a cheap cup of coffee could be bought for US$1.50.

Tae would read and apply ideas from other industries, such as fashion and apparel chain stores, on how they interacted with their customers, as he felt that more could be learnt across industries rather than by visiting competing coffee shops. He observed that the retail business was very dynamic, with new products brought in every three to six months. Hence, on a weekly basis, Tae would introduce a new 'Coffee of the Week', specifying the country and region it was from, so that customers could try something different. He explained, "When it comes to retail, it's always about branding communication. We want customers to truly feel that they are getting more than just a simple cup of coffee".

Rebranding

When the first Alto store was set up, the symbol of an owl was chosen for its logo as it was easy for anyone to identify with. Also, owls did not sleep at night — an association with the idea of drinking coffee and staying awake. The Alto Coffee logo was used on all of its marketing materials and coffee cups, and the font was such that it emphasised 'Alto' as a concept and not 'coffee' (the latter was in significantly smaller font to the former). Customers walking into an Alto Coffee outlet would see a wall with cartoons of 12 owls with different facial expressions.

While the owl seemed like a good idea, it was abandoned four years later in March 2016, with the third store opening (after which the first two stores were also redone). Research showed that the shop and owl logo was perceived as warm and friendly, but not associated with a premium coffee specialist experience. The company then instituted a rebranding process with a new logo and corporate identity using a more masculine dark blue décor. Sales jumped immediately, and it registered an estimated 12% growth from the rebranding change in the first six months.

The Wholesale Side

When Alto first started wholesale operations, much of its resources were spent securing distributor rights for a European coffee machine brand. Tae spent US$80,000 in the first two years on procuring and promoting these machines at various trade shows. The initial idea was to sell these machines and wholesale coffees to other cafes and businesses. For a small company with just one store at that time, these sunk costs affected the cash flow and slowed down any expansion plan tremendously. To make matters worse, the distributorship policy was later changed and Alto had to give up the importing rights to a much larger coffee company. Alto had to then take on as many new customers as possible without any particular sub-segment in mind to keep the wholesale business together.

The wholesale segment was attractive to Tae because those customers would buy as many as 50 to 100 bags of coffee each time, while the retail ones would invariably purchase only one or two bags of coffee at a time. However, wholesale selling was less about marketing value and more about price. While retail coffee prices are largely based on the value of limited availability and origins, wholesale coffees adopt cost-based pricing as the customers are more price-sensitive given that the coffee beans are used as an ingredient in their businesses. While Alto's coffee beans ranged from US$19.50 to US$53.50 per kilogram, one of their most popular signature blends was selling at US$30 per kilogram. In the market, it was common to find standard grade coffee beans priced from US$9.60–US$19.30, and some, like Illy, an established international coffee wholesaler, was priced at US$64.20 per kilogram.

Over time, Tae decided that targeting high-end cafes and restaurants could be profitable and that with the firm's approach to quality and cost structure, the low price point market was not really an option. Thus, Tae wanted to gear Alto's communication towards attracting this segment. Alto decided not to entertain businesses who tried to bargain on price and did not recognise that they needed to pay a premium for quality coffee. As Tae explained, "When our customers do not understand why they are paying more for our coffees, chances are they are not committed to quality. This will cause a problem for us in the long run".

Although wholesale customers were sensitive to the price of the coffee beans, Tae still found ways to provide value and justify the premium price. For F&B customers who were opening their own cafes and restaurants, Alto positioned itself as a solution provider with a training program for the staff on how to make coffee, as well as offer them other free support services such as customising their menus. He even advised them on cost control management. On the day that a new shop opened, Tae and his team would be on-site to make sure that the operation and other processes went smoothly. Tae's belief was, "The better our customers do, the better Alto does".

Customers who opened their own cafes did not see Alto as a competitor. In fact, some of them would source cheaper coffee beans from different suppliers as their base menu, and sell Alto's blend as a premium upgrade at a higher price. There was no binding agreement between Alto and its customers on how the coffee must be prepared. Rather, customers were taught to fine-tune their equipment to create a unique taste for their own cafes, as the same coffee would taste different with various settings. Due to so many factors affecting quality control, customers were not permitted to place the Alto logo in their own cafes.

The Road Ahead

For the first three years after the opening of the Megabangna cafe, Alto had not reached the sales targets it had set for itself. As a new local specialty coffee brand, it took time to gain brand awareness and many customers were slow to acquire a palette for fruity or chocolate-tone coffees as they were used to drinking bitter coffees. However, sales began to pick up and increased after the rebranding process. Tae estimated that each new café outlet would take 28 to 36 months to break even. By the end of 2018, the annual revenue was expected to be around US$750,000.

Having been able to develop a growing customer base and a reputation as a best-in-class supplier, the future looks bright for Alto. Their proposition to retail and wholesale customers has been refined and put in place. Yet Tae commented, "I think our performance has a lot of room to improve. We're always looking to grow the business. Even if our cafes are full, we are not happy. There's no way I can grow the business unless we continue to do other things. I'm not very easily satisfied".

Chapter 11

THAI HABEL INDUSTRIAL CO. LTD: WHEN A FIRE IGNITES A CHANGE OF DIRECTION AND UNDERPINS EXPANSION

The Thai Habel Industrial Co. Ltd. is a specialised manufacturer of popular home audio-visual products and small appliances. Established in 1987 by the late Pornthep S., an engineer, Thai Habel was the country's first television set manufacturer and later went on to make the country's first colour television set. However, in 2015, disaster struck in the form of a devastating factory fire. Yet the loss of nearly seventy percent of the factory's floor space proved to be the unlikely catalyst behind the company's current success, underpinned by an astute three-pronged sequence of strategies and tactics that included a harnessing of Thailand's Free Trade Agreements. Three years later, Deputy Managing Director, Narindej Thaveesangpanich, who was brought in to turn the company around, says he is confident that the company's focus on "strength from within" will lay the groundwork for its future expansion into other countries as well as Thailand itself.

When the founder of Thai Habel Industrial Co. Ltd., Pornthep S., launched the country's first manufacturer of Cathode Ray Tube TVs,[1] or CRT TVs as they are known, it was an older type of display technology, and in 2018 it was rarely ever encountered in many parts of the world. Established in 1987, the company is headquartered in Bangkok and has two factories located in Prachinburi and Nakornpathom.

In 1992, Thai Habel became the distributor of Sampo Corp., the Taiwanese manufacturer of radios and televisions. In the years that followed, the company was basically an Original Equipment Manufacturer (OEM) for a lot of brands. OEM products are those items that are sold in bulk to manufacturers and usually tagged on items that are less expensive than normal retail products. In addition to Liquid Crystal Display (LCD) and Light Emitting Diode (LED) televisions, the company also manufactured, and continues to this day to make, rice cookers and electric kettles, both under its own brands as well as an OEM manufacturer for major modern trade and B2B websites such as Tesco Lotus, Big C, Makro, Do Home, and Mega Home, as well as for online markets like Lazada, Shopee, and WeMall. It sells and distributes throughout Thailand and also exports across various regions such as Indochina, India, and the Middle East.

The company began to produce its own house brands in the year 2000, but in 2010, an enormous change occurred with the arrival of the multinational giant retailer Tesco, which had a huge capacity and lots of stores nationwide. "We started our own brand, and they selected us. Our sales were very good and we kept growing until 2014", recalled Deputy Managing Director, Narindej Thaveesangpanich, better known as Jack, who, at that stage, was yet to join the company.

By 2013 the company had decided to start its own brand, although it was not a rebranded one, said Jack. "We decided to do this because we had started to engage with the modern trade, which is always looking for a house brand, and which can also be problematic. In the case of Makro, for example, the trademark for the house brand belongs to them. But for Tesco, they requested us to do the trademark registration. The brand belonged to us, but they requested us to be in that single channel only. So it's not really a brand. It's sort of a house brand that is held captive by the store or channel you sell through. But this also depends on who owns the trademark. In short, I'd just call it a 'house brand'.

Technically known as 'controlled brands', such OEM registered brands are exclusive. Even though the Thai Habel Group owns them, the retailer controls them and is the only one allowed to resell it. The reason for this is that the retailer has a real incentive to support these kind of brands because they are the only ones who sell them, which means they are free from within brand competition; they do not want to put something under their own name because they do not want potential service problems and customer complaint issues. As Jack explained, "When they're seeking a toehold in the market, they will sometimes go in this direction and will want someone else to help them build a brand, but they realise they're in control of the brand".

In 2015, a devastating fire swept through the company's major factory, putting all future plans on hold.

The Fire and Family Ties

The fire that destroyed approximately seventy percent of the company's factory burned continuously for nine hours, the consequence of the actions of a disgruntled employee, who was later jailed. Financially, the company had to bear the brunt of a US$6 million loss — it was not covered by insurance. Furthermore, due to legal considerations, it was not possible to rebuild the factory as the fire had gone on for more than six hours. As Jack recounts, "This meant the company had to start from scratch, demolish everything including the floor. The size of the investment was prohibitive, and ultimately the company decided to focus on the existing smaller second plant that we had mostly used as a warehouse and distribution centre".

"My wife and her younger brother, who were running the company, came to me. 'Hey Jack, can you help me?' She was the eldest daughter of the founder. So what could I do?" Jack agreed to join but under certain stipulations.

A marketing professional and graduate of Thammasat University's Master's in Marketing (MIM) programme, Jack had the skillset to provide an expert perspective. He had previously worked with leading Thai companies, the CP Group and Central, and later joined the government, reporting directly to the Prime Minister's office. The experience gained in international markets, trade, import and export, and high-level government perspectives was invaluable. He later joined Thailand's largest market activation agency, called Index Creative Village.

His demands were straightforward: "I told them that if I have to sacrifice my high salary, then I will ask for only two things. The first is to do export, which they'd never done before. I knew that we were badly in need of cash flow, and export was the quickest solution. The second was for us to have our own brand, a real brand".

Jack passionately recalled, "The branding was important. The company couldn't survive otherwise. We couldn't do OEM all the time because its margins are very slim as we only make money on the assembly parts. So to make the company sustainable we had to make our own brand. I think I got this right because later on a lot of people actually trusted us to produce their own brands". There was only one catch, he advised them. Branding meant a big change, from the inside as well as the obvious external changes. "The employees also had to change, and there were the complexities of a family-run business to consider as well".

Organisational rebranding took place. The company logo was changed — which also meant employees could see tangible results, Jack recalled, along with exploring market diversification. "We were doing OEM for TVs, but we began to do this for home appliances as well. What I was trying to do was to utilise every single product I could because I had a lot of factory lines. It was a case of anything I could do to make money".

Management issues were also at the fore, including changing the mind-set of the people inside the organisation, and getting them to act professionally. "It might be basic management principles, but I also think the Thai people, and a lot of family business people, struggle with it. If they don't act professionally then it's still like a family business. I cleaned it all out and put in place the rules of professional behaviour".

The change management process was not easy. "I couldn't just get rid of nonperformers because they had been so loyal to the company. But they were also quite old — the youngest was around forty, while I was thirty-eight — they couldn't speak English, although I couldn't mention that to them. I used to speak English a lot. But once I came here, I had to change everything to Thai because I had to communicate with them".

There was more. "Not only were they relatively old, they were also very old-time. They didn't know how to Google, for example, so I had to teach them. I started with a closed Facebook group and put all of them in it. Even so, my team had to do everything, including how to register. We did this every week, with a campaign every month. I used a reward system for questionnaires in order to test them on the company's history. I'd ask them when the company was established, for which they'd respond with 'the day The Terminator came out' or 'the day our boxers became world champions.' It wasn't necessarily straightforward. I was encouraging them to use Google to find the answer".

It wasn't an easy task. There were already many international players, Jack said, and he needed to do something with the Thais in mind. "I challenged them. 'If you are Thai, what are the good things about being Thai?'"

Finances Post-Fire

Faced with recouping some, if not all, of the US$6 million loss was a challenge. Post-fire reconstruction, the company decided to focus on maximum utilisation of its existing facilities rather than building new ones. In 2017, the company had just covered its losses, with Jack setting aside funds for bonuses to thank the staff that had been there since the fire as well as for product development. He also made the decision to take the company's distribution centre in-house.

Nowadays, company revenue is two-fold: one is from the OEM side, he said, which is the core business. The other is from branding. "But right now I would say my branding with Altron exceeds the income from OEM".

On the corporate turn-around, he said he never actually felt it. "To be honest, I felt I'd jumped into the wrong pool. I went from a professional job to doing everything with no time to rest. And I had to learn it all myself".

His competitors, however, said he had changed the industry. Local brands began to be advertised and emotional branding campaigns — previously never heard of — were introduced. "Having asked the employees 'what are the good things about being Thai?' was starting to show up in our design, our promotion, and our image in the market". Copycat branding took this one step further.

Interestingly, at the beginning of 2016, after the launch of Altron, Jack discovered that his competitors were also launching a Thai brand. "What's interesting here is that they've been in the market for thirty years and all the while they have been claiming their products are from the United States. Once they saw our success, they said they were also Thai brands. So that's one indicator that we did it right".

The Launch of Altron

Prior to the launch of Altron, leading international brands were in the throes of penetrating the high-end market while no-name brand products from China held sway in the low-end market. There was a gap, Jack explained, in the middle to lower end of the market, which meant Thai Habel could penetrate the market by leveraging its production capacity and its kudos as a trusted and certified brand endorsed by many organisations (most notably the Thailand Trust Mark and the Prime Ministers Award). At the same time, there was a growing nationalist sentiment on the part of Thai customers, who were proud to be Thai, and had full confidence in the quality of Thai products assembled in Thai factories for Thai people. To characterise this period, the wind began to fill the sails and the sales began to rise.

Launched in November 2015, one year after the fire, Thai Habel introduced its Altron TV in more than 166 branches of TESCO Lotus countrywide. The launch was very successful, garnering 81 items of media coverage. The reason for that, he said, was that they were the first ones to dare to use the "Made in Thailand brand". None of the others that were made in Thailand stood out, he recalled.

The high point of Altron's success involved Jack's decision to utilise third party endorsements as a marketing strategy. It paid off: "I know that I'm going to have a lot of questions and that no one is going to believe me. I told them: 'Yes I understand, and that's why I have the Thailand Trust mark from the ministry and so many awards to back me up. Talk to our government because they actually endorsed us.'"

The Altron product is a high quality LED product that is designed to meet the needs of consumers and is in response to the competition in the TV market. Available in six hundred outlets across Thailand as well as online, its features include a simple and contemporary design, easy-to-use functions, and a three-year warranty, with more than one hundred and eighty-five authorised service centres across Thailand.

Altron TV products target the C+ to B Socio Economic Status (SES) demographic, which measures an individual's or family's economic and social position in relation to others, based on income, education, and occupation. Its customers are generally aged between 18 and 65.

Targeting this demographic, where the company is seeking to become the first player at the leading edge of the electronic industry, is generally a rich person's game, where they will play primarily for the high C and middle B market. Occasionally, they get to the A market, but as a secondary target. To play for the A market, said Jack, you have to be on the leading edge of the technology. "We made the decision not to be the technology leader. But when the technology becomes more stable, at a lower cost, and lower priced, we can play in that space".

Altron alone now represents around three percent of the market. "It sounds small, but the market is around THB 31,000 billion, so it's quite huge", he added.

While products are available online, Jack is not chasing e-commerce by drawing traffic to the company's website. "I think it's better to use other third-party platforms and let them do the drawing of traffic". Ideally, he continues, "For e-commerce to be healthy, it should constitute ten percent of the whole portfolio. At present we only have one or two percent, which is still very small. That might be due to established competitor's historic brand advantage or price wars. When the big brands do online sales, they bring the prices way down. Very, very remarkable prices".

Branding and the Battle for Credibility

The other side of branding saw Jack pull out all stops to build trust in his new brand. "Now if I went out and said 'Hey these products made in Thailand are of very good quality', no one would have believed me. My battle was to make the Thai people proud that their country had a decent Thai brand that was not only bringing out good, high-quality products, but also the best service. These days that's changed and Thai brands seem to carry prestige when they go to places like Myanmar, Vietnam, Cambodia, and Laos".

The keystone in his corporate and marketing strategy was to utilise third party endorsement, which would later underpin several creative marketing tactics. Third party endorsements included certification by various agencies such as ISO, the Thai Industrial Standards Institute, a green industry rating for the factory, a category five energy-efficiency label from the Ministry of Energy, the Thailand Trust Mark from the Ministry of Commerce, and the Prime Minister's Award for export (after the company began to export to India and Bangladesh).

He started his quest for endorsements well ahead of the launch of Altron, using the emotional connection between Thai people to Thai brands. "Our brand is made in Thailand and my product is good enough. If I don't do this, the Ministry of Commerce won't endorse me".

"The Thailand Trust mark award was a great success", he said, "and provided an interesting twist down in the weeds on a traditional public relations tactic. We had a chance to showcase ourselves at an exhibition where the Prime Minister was due to come by our booth. I used to work for him before so I knew all the ways to attract him to the booth. I told the team right away the minute I got the call from the director of the Ministry of Commerce at nine in the evening. 'Hey Jack,' he said, 'tomorrow you have to be there because the Prime Minister will walk to your booth.' Naturally I said OK".

A light bulb moment flashed. "I needed the free PR. Most people would have just been happy to have the photo opportunity with the Prime Minister and show the product. But I thought we have to do something different, something more creative. So once he arrived, I showed him the products. I had a television with the Altron logo that was on display and before he left the booth, I said to him, 'Can I have your autograph?' Very simple, right? 'Where's your paper?' he asked. But I didn't have any paper. Instead, I gave him a permanent marker and he autographed the Altron TV. 'On the TV?' he said. Right. Naturally the media took many photos. The coverage was fantastic".

A second strategy involved leveraging Thailand's Free Trade Agreements (FTA) and is an important part of the firm's overall plans. "If you want to export, there are only two points that you need to overcome. One is pricing, which sees you compete with the Chinese. Another is an advantage on tax or tariffs".

Take Daewoo, for example, the top brand of Korea, he said. "We actually produce for them here. And we export to Vietnam. Because I understand all about the FTAs, I will search for people that will bring us more advantage in terms of tariffs and everything. So I'll talk to them and say 'hey, let's do it here.' And you have 'Made in Thailand' which means you get a valuable brand at a reasonable or reduced tariff".

A third element involves strategic partnerships. Jack introduced a Video on Demand (VOD) application, "just like Netflix, but local". The local VOD collaborated with Sony, Panasonic, and Samsung by initially giving out free limited days of subscription — but it didn't work out well because the complexity of the smart TV made it hard to get the VOD app right. "I therefore offered them a shortcut button right on the remote that allowed consumers to access thousands of movies easily, and also improved the chance of getting subscriptions renewed. Now they are our strategic partners. For every smart TV that comes out, we are able to offer our customers a free ninety-day subscription. In return, they get their brand promoted on our remote, for which they are very happy".

Tactics

In 2018, Jack said the company would be focusing more on after sales services. "We've been here for two years already and both the price and the brand have been getting higher and higher. It helps the company's marketing effort, for which the budget is not great. What we have actually spent in the last two years would surprise you", he said.

Its Facebook account offers exclusive items for its fans; the "Thai Listen Test", whose message "Thai brands can do more than you ever thought" proved enormously effective. Meanwhile the company's Euro-Cup campaign brought promotions to a whole new level.

"It involved some big fish for us", he said. It was also the first time Thai Habel had ventured into sports marketing. "The reason I did this is because I knew I had to reach people who could return the money to me very quickly. I couldn't go everywhere and I had to be very specific. At that time the Thai soccer team was very popular and I was about to promote my Thai Listen products. It was the only way to reach these people". He did roadshows with them when, for example, Manchester United were playing against Leicester City. "I got my brand in that market as well. While Manchester United was the most popular of all of them, Leicester City was owned by a Thai", he said in reference to Thai billionaire, Vichai Srivaddhanaprabha, who made his fortune operating a network of duty-free shops and bought the club in 2010.[2] Leicester City achieved its greatest success when it won the 2015–2016 Premier League as a 5,000/1 underdog.

Jack also sponsored the Miss Thailand contest, one of his emotion-based campaigns advocating "Support the beauty of Thais". The company also ran a Corporate Social Responsibility (CSR) campaign in the troubled south of Thailand. Jack personally brought the televisions down there, with the crew from the Miss Thailand event. Together, they endorsed his message: "Altron: Thai TV for Thais is very proud to support the three provinces in southern Thailand. We would like all of you to send your support to our brotherhood together".

The company also launched a program aimed at Thailand's senior generation when it created a large print, simplified remote control.

Due to be launched on the King's birthday in 2016, he postponed the campaign as the King passed away, re-launching it later as a memorial to the King. "We gave it away for free".

Where Eagles Dare to Fly

Above all, we wanted the Altron brand to be recognised as a brand that dedicates its products and services to the Thai people, Jack noted. "Before the launch of my own TV brand, I analysed the market to ensure there was no gap left. All the big names and big international players were already here in Thailand. A lot of Indians came here in the last two years just to buy a TV and bring it back home. This was an indicator that the cheapest television market is in Thailand".

There were several preliminary issues to be resolved. These included the possibility of fluctuation in the demand for OEMs, which saw him diversify the market. "I captured the local market first. This was my core. Then exports to India, for example, are another part, and its seasonal demand might not be the same with Thailand's in terms of selling. On the other hand, I also have Vietnam. So I have three markets together so I can balance the production line".

But there were times when he admits that he couldn't control the line because of fluctuations in the cost of raw materials. "Sometimes the costs went sky high, which meant I might not be able to export during that time. Then there were currency issues".

Expanding Its Wings

Pre-fire, Thai Habel had around one hundred employees, including at the factory. Now there were seven hundred, making it a moderately large company.

The Thai Habel Industrial Co. and its Altron TV brand is now setting its sights on the introduction of three more series to provide customers with more options. "We will turn Altron into our major brand, accounting for forty percent of total company sales volume and penetrate the international market, including expansion into the regional market", he announced recently.

He is aiming for Vietnam in particular, and said he wants to see it become one of Vietnam's best-known brands within five years. "Fortunately, 'Made in Thailand' is well known in neighbouring countries, especially in Vietnam, and we will be leveraging ourselves to transform this as our key strength to compete with global rivals".

Already well-established in Laos, Altron has accessed Myanmar and Cambodia mainly via border trade. Its other international export markets have included South Africa, India, Morocco, South America, and the Middle East.

As to projections for the overall market right now, he said, it was a difficult call. The markets have been slow since the passing of His Majesty King Bhumibol Adulyadej in 2016, however the "Shop to help the nation" campaign did well enough to stimulate spending in the very last period of 2016. "I would rather wait and see a bit more. What I can see now is that the home-appliances market will keep growing, with audio-visual appliances either remaining stable or perhaps growing very slightly".

His next key challenge will be to face the intensity of the competition. "Our goals are to continue migrating the product and product mix, to stay fresh, and to come up with new products and new categories. Further, to access more international markets while continuing to farm the Thai market".

But to be honest, he adds, "I just want to diversify the risk. The television industry has grown and we still have plenty of channels to expand. People are starting to trust our brand. And of course Altron is not only a TV brand, but is also entering the digital signage sector".

"The only way is up", Jack says, confidently.

Endnotes

1. CRT stands for Cathode-Ray Tube. It is an older type of display technology going back more than a decade. If you can picture an old school computer with a big case, you can picture a CRT display. In order to create a picture on a CRT monitor, scientists fashioned the system to take advantage of the attraction between negatively charged cathodes and a positively charged anodes when electricity is introduced. When doing so, beams of light are shot at a display screen, which is coated in phosphor. This phosphor can display light in different colors, and the system harnesses this ability to create a picture.
2. South China Morning Post, "Vichai Srivaddhanaprabha: the Thai-Chinese billionaire behind Leicester City's English Premier League fairytale", 29 October 2018, https://www.scmp.com/sport/football/article/2170601/.

SECTION 4: Making it big: Success against all odds

Finally, no book on an entrepreneur's journey in Thailand would be complete without looking at William (Bill) Heinecke and the Minor Group. Heinecke's management philosophy has been "to find passion and joy in whatever you do". Beginning his entrepreneurial journey just shy of his eighteenth birthday, Heinecke opened the Inter-Asian Enterprise and Inter-Asian Publicity, selling advertising by day and using a mop and bucket to clean offices in the evening. From those early days, the multi-billion dollar Minor Group was founded, and is a name to be reckoned with inside and outside Thailand. Heinecke's recommended strategy for sucess: learn to spot the right opportunities at the right time, go international, recruit and nurture talented people, and, most of all, build the ability to overcome crises. As he says, "Entrepreneurship teaches you resilience, so learn from it."

Chapter 12

MINOR INTERNATIONAL: COMPETING ON THE WORLD STAGE

Born-entrepreneur, William 'Bill' Heinecke has built one of the largest hospitality, food and leisure groups in Asia. What have been the keys to success?

Are entrepreneurs born or made? That is an oft-asked question and the answer invariably is that they could be either. William 'Bill' Heinecke's is, however, a case of being both. Born to be an entrepreneur, Heinecke's story over five decades is one of triumph punctuated with tribulations. It is a story of an American-born youngster who became a Thai citizen and made it big, first in Thailand and then across Asia and other parts of the world. And it is very much a story of resilience — of failures, setbacks and crises that paved the way to new ideas, new learnings and ultimately, successes.

Heinecke came to Thailand as a child and started his first business before he turned 18; hence naming his company Minor International. A Thai citizen since 1991, today, he oversees 513 hotels and resorts, more than 2,000 restaurants and 400 retail stores, spread across 62 countries. Minor's portfolio includes hotel brands such as Anantara, Four Seasons, St Regis and Portugal's Tivoli, and also franchises for well-known western brands, such as Swensen's, Sizzler, Dairy Queen and Burger King. And Heinecke and the group show no signs of slowing down, as they tripled the size of the hotel portfolio by acquiring Spain's NH Hotels for US$2.6 billion in 2018. Today, Minor is one of the largest hotel, food and retail companies in the world, with a significant and rapidly expanding presence in over 60 markets across Asia, Australasia, the Middle East, Africa, the Indian Ocean, Europe and the Americas. Clearly, a world away from the office cleaning and advertising companies that he started as a 17-year-old in Bangkok, Thailand.

Seeds of Entrepreneurship

Born to Roy and Connie Heinecke in Virginia, United States in 1949, Heinecke became a Thai citizen in 1991. A year after Heinecke was born, his father Roy left for Tokyo to work for the U.S. Marine Corps. Choosing not to be left behind, Connie, with only $60 to spare, booked tickets on a tramp steamer and arrived with her two sons in the Japanese port of Sasebo about a month later. In 1963, when he was 14 years old, Heinecke moved to Bangkok, having previously lived in Japan, Hong Kong and Malaysia.

Heinecke's entrepreneurial skills showed up quite early. He set up a lemonade stand in nursery school and at the age of ten started assisting at a café run by an old couple who had befriended him. He commenced his career as a 14-year old writer for the English daily, Bangkok World, writing columns about go-karting. The editor agreed to publish the columns and pay him only on the condition that he would secure advertisements to run alongside. Go-kart suppliers in Bangkok took a keen interest in the promotion opportunity and ads began to pour in. The regular stream of ads ensured that Heinecke's columns became a regular feature of the newspaper, and soon he started writing advertising supplements about motor cars. When the advertising manager quit, Heinecke who had been acting as his unofficial deputy, began to make his mark, selling advertising space for the newspaper.

In 1967, a high school graduate, Heinecke received an offer to pursue his higher studies at Georgetown University in Washington — which he declined, to the dismay of his parents. Instead, he took a loan of 25,000 Ticals (baht) and simultaneously set up a cleaning and an advertising business. The Inter-Asian Enterprise and Inter-Asian Publicity, over the course of the next 35 years, grew to become Minor International (MINT), one of the leading international concerns in the hospitality and lifestyle sectors employing more than 66,000 people in its branches in 6 continents across the globe.

By the age of 21, Heinecke was a millionaire. Soon after, in the early 1970s, the advertising giant Ogilvy & Mather (O&M) entered the Asian market and opened an office in Thailand. However, it had no ears on the ground, and so was interested in the advertising wing of Heinecke's corporation. O&M proceeded to acquire 100 per cent of Inter-Asian Publicity, and Heinecke, as Managing Director of the acquired firm, got an opportunity to gain insights into the intricate workings of an advertising concern.

It is with this rather illustrious backdrop that Minor International (MINT), in just over five decades, has become a major player in Asia-Pacific. After imprinting its presence in the region, the group has slowly but steadily grown to other parts of the world including Africa, the Middle East, Europe and the US.

Heinecke's management philosophy has been to "find passion and joy in whatever you do". When he's not overseeing his far-flung marketing, manufacturing, food, property and hotel development activities, he can be found piloting his airplane or indulging in other passions such as scuba diving and racing antique sport cars — all passions that were at times a part of the Minor empire. 2019 saw him turning 70 years of age, but the passion and the business continues to drive him. What are the success factors of MINT? What are the lessons for other entrepreneurs from Heinecke's life and career?

Four Keys to Success

Spot the Right Opportunities at the Right Time

Thailand's changing economy spearheaded by rapid industrialisation was creating a middle class with disposable incomes. Heinecke had a hunch that it was time to introduce the Thais to American fast food, and that their sweet tooth was the first thing to aim at. He conceived the idea of bringing the Mister Donut franchise to the country, and the first Mister Donut outlet opened in 1975. That became a model for franchising for the group in the years to come.

In 1978, Heinecke resigned from the chairmanship of O&M to devote his full attention to Minor Holdings. The first fruit of this concentration of energy was a hotel venture in Pattaya. Long familiar with Pattaya as a vacation spot, Heinecke had noted the decline of a hotel there formerly used by the US military for its troops on R&R (rest and recuperation) leave from the Vietnam War (which had ended in 1975). In 1976, Minor took over the operation of the property on a 25-year lease agreement with the landlord, Sribathana Co. Ltd. Minor comprehensively renovated and remodelled the property and reopened it as the Royal Garden Resort in 1978 — a small step that eventually became a giant leap, as the name Royal Garden Resorts (RGR) was pinned to an ever-expanding hotel group now known as Minor Hotels.

Destined to be another major component of the group, Minor Food was founded in 1980 as Heinecke foresaw rapid growth in the coming decade in this market sector. Given Thailand's new and growing consumer society and the arrival of multi-storey shopping malls based on the American pattern, Minor Food saw the opportunity to expand the restaurant franchising that it had begun in 1975 with Mister Donut. That American bakery concept was enjoying success, and so Heinecke felt the time was ripe to introduce the Thais to American fast food. He chose Pizza Hut to begin with, but the announcement of the deal was met with surprise in the business community. People said it would never work, that Thais do not like cheese — many are lactose intolerant — and the pizza outlets would fail, but Heinecke pressed ahead. The first restaurant opened in Pattaya, at the same seaside location as Minor's first hotel, the Royal Garden Resort. The franchise for Thailand had been bought for US$5,000, plus a royalty on all sales, and it proved an excellent investment. The first restaurant was a roaring success and there soon followed a second, third and fourth outlet, all three located in Bangkok.

With the Thais' sweet appetite already proven at Mister Donut, the company's next set of franchises were Swensen's, and then the soft serve ice cream specialist Dairy Queen.

Think Big, Go Global

Over the years, Minor had dipped into some ventures outside its home market of Thailand. It launched the Haiphong Harbour View Hotel (now AVANI Hai Phong Harbour View) in Vietnam in 1998 and The Pizza Company in Kuwait in 2002. During 2005–2008, the company made several bold overseas investments as part of a strategy to further international expansion. In early 2005, it rebranded itself as Minor International (MINT), marking the beginning of an exciting new phase in its history, as a larger, more diversified and more international enterprise.

As a result of the above, Minor's international revenue increased by 119 per cent compared to 2004, with the company collecting fee revenues from businesses in seven countries compared to only three in the previous year. In 2005, Minor made what was at the time its largest international investment, allocating THB 480 million (over US$12 million at the time) to finance the construction of three resorts in the Maldives and expand its food business in China.

In fact, Minor's first attempt at entering the Chinese market had taken place nearly two decades earlier. In 1989, Minor made an investment to launch Pizza Hut in China, but eventually sold the business. Although the venture was short-lived, the company had played a part in pioneering fast food in the country. In 2005, Minor re-entered the market with five outlets of The Pizza Company and four Sizzler restaurants in Beijing, in partnership with Beijing Le Jazz Catering Co., Ltd.

In 2005, The Pizza Company added 12 new outlets in Thailand and 13 internationally as the brand was introduced in the UAE, Cambodia and the Philippines. By the end of 2005, there were 164 The Pizza Company outlets operating globally, 146 of them in Thailand, 5 in China and 13 elsewhere. Significantly, in December 2005, Minor also signed an agreement with Kayla Foods, the owner of the Swensen's brand, to expand its franchise and sub-franchise rights from 19 countries to over 30 worldwide, including India.

Commented Heinecke, "Following on from the difficult times of the tsunami in January 2004, we began to grow abroad in a big way because we realised the need for diversification in terms of business and also geography. Spread yourself out so you are not going to be hit by one thing that can be as devastating as a tsunami or a 1997 Asian financial crisis. So we moved into the Maldives, one of our first international operations, and started making investments in Sri Lanka, Tanzania and Kenya. We invested more in Vietnam, Australia and Singapore, and those markets began to really grow. Today we have very diversified businesses across a broad geography. We run the gamut of real estate investments from three-star hotels all the way to six-star properties. We also started developing shopping centres, residential developments and office complexes alongside our hotels".

People Make All the Difference

Minor's fast pace of growth meant that its leadership team played a key part in role-modelling the company's vision and perpetuating the 'Drive' culture — recruiting and nurturing talented people to take on board this culture, lifting their own capabilities and driving the company forward at the same time. While conceding that leadership can be an elusive quality to define, Heinecke gave some tips in *The Entrepreneur* that hint at the kind of leaders he would want to bring into the business.[1] These include:

- Motivate people by making them understand the importance of their job
- Trust your team, so that they give you full effort in return
- Stay cool under pressure, so that those around you feel confident
- Be an expert, so that your staff see that you know what you are talking about
- Be a good listener, so that your staff feel free to come up with ideas.

Sums up Heinecke, "I was a great believer that some of these things just couldn't fail, but what I realised is that businesses are very much dependent on the people operating them. So if you do not have the right people, even though you may have a good idea and a good brand, it is not necessarily going to work. Therefore, you quickly learn that people are more important than the brand because even big brands can fail in a market. That is when you start developing your HR skills. Suddenly, we're paying a lot more attention to recruiting people, who we partner with, and who we do business with — because it really makes a huge difference".

In 1998, there began a titanic battle for the future of Thailand's American-style pizza restaurant segment, dominated by Pizza Hut. With its Pizza Hut sales experiencing little growth, Minor decided to branch into the fried chicken business. After PepsiCo, the then-owner of KFC that also owned Pizza Hut, declined Minor's offer to operate KFC restaurants in either Thailand or elsewhere in Asia, Minor signed an agreement with Chicken Treat, an Australian chicken brand, to develop the Thai, Malaysian and Singaporean markets. Minor's franchise agreement with Pizza Hut at the time only restricted the Company from running another pizza brand, so this should not have been an issue. However, when the agreement came up for renewal in 1998, Minor was presented with radically new terms.

Without any warning, on 17 November 1999, Tricon placed full-page notices in three leading Thai newspapers publicly revealing the state of its negotiations with Minor and giving a deadline of 17 January 2000 for Minor to agree to its terms or else Tricon would operate Pizza Hut in Thailand itself. The company's share price fell by 25 per cent on that same day and by over 50% in the next 30 days. Over US$50 million in shareholder value evaporated in that time, and then the banks started calling to cut the company's credit lines. Many entrepreneurs would have called it a day and bowed to the power of a global giant — but not Heinecke. Having invested so much in Pizza Hut's success and loath to abandon all the pizza making and marketing expertise the company had acquired, he decided to fight back with Minor's own brand of pizza.

When the Pizza Hut brand licence ended, Minor had a hiatus of 45 days to get its new brand up and running. Benefitting from immense staff commitment (nobody quit to join the new Pizza Hut outfit), and some imaginative recipes, a new pizza brand called The Pizza Company launched in 116 locations across Thailand on 17 March 2001.

The key to Minor's success in the pizza restaurant business, Heinecke concluded, was not the brand name but the staff who had built up Pizza Hut and who now worked for The Pizza Company. "While a powerful tool, a brand is only as good as the people using it", Heinecke wrote. "In a nutshell, people build brands, brands don't build people". By the end of 2005, The Pizza Company had 146 outlets in Thailand and had branched out overseas with a further 18 outlets. The Thai Prime Minister at the time, Thaksin Shinawatra, famously took a large party to dine at The Pizza Company in Chiang Mai in August 2002, providing high-profile publicity for the brand. The Pizza Wars were overcome with victory to Heinecke.

Build Resilience, Overcome Crises

In July 1997, SEA was hit by the worst financial crisis since the post-colonisation era. Currencies collapsed, stock markets and other assets were severely devalued, there was a steep rise in private debt and economies spiralled. And in the thick of it all was the Land of Smiles. Thailand's prospering economy came to a halt. Massive layoffs in finance, real estate and construction resulted in huge numbers of workers returning to their villages in the countryside and more than half a million foreign workers sent back to their native countries. 53 percent of Thai bank loans were classified as non-performing, and in a matter of weeks, the nation's currency melted down from 25 baht to the dollar to 56 baht to the dollar.

One of the few companies in Thailand that stood strong through it all was The Minor Group. Heinecke was one of the few businesspersons who acted early and minimised the losses. However, overcoming the challenge did not come about without a struggle, as the group scaled down its operations and had to lay off several employees, some of whom had served the business for over a decade. But times were tough and tough decisions had to be made. Heinecke froze bonuses and raises for all senior staff and began reducing the non-performing 20 percent of the staff. Menu items in the food businesses were reduced to meet the needs of an increasingly value conscious consumer and the hotel business started pricing rooms in dollars, not Baht, to reduce the company's exposure to a declining local currency.

The 1997 Asian crisis was a sobering time for Minor, but the lessons learned prepared them for a bright future. Having to cut costs and let go of people, even those who had been with the company for over a decade, taught them to be resilient and proactive at a time of impending crisis. Heinecke added, "At that time, we never thought about this as an opportunity for a management refocus, but upon reflection we saw the need to maintain high-performers and that a culture of high performers could lead us. In essence, that's when we sort of hit on the fact that we better figure out how to continue growing, and we're only going to do that if we can retain and reward great people. The Asian Financial Crisis had a lasting positive effect on the way we did business. If we had stayed without cutting that 20 percent, then for sure we could not afford to pay any more money to our high performers. As a matter of fact, everybody would probably make a little bit less. Then pretty soon, the good people would leave because they wanted to better themselves. So you'd lose your best people".

In Heinecke's words: "Entrepreneurship teaches you resilience, so learn from it. It isn't over until you say it's over. But know when to call it quits. One of the mistakes we often make is that we think we can make things right. And in the old days, we prided ourselves on that... but sometimes you have to recognize what made you — and one of the things that made us successful was this willingness to shut something down quickly when it wasn't working".

The resilience and the inbuilt quality of his enterprise saw Minor through several more major disasters, such as the 2004 tsunami, the outbreak of bird flu, and political upheavals that affected the tourism and lifestyle industries, the backbone of Minor's operations.

Looking Ahead

Optimistic of the future, says Heinecke, "I am very bullish, especially about ASEAN. You can't get away from the European Union, America, China, Brexit and other trade complexities. Africa is the only region where I still feel we are pioneering. I think if you want to see a new China, then you have to look at Africa. They've got the mineral wealth, human capital, and a developing education sector. And it is undeveloped and untapped. Russia also has potential, and while it has had its ups and downs, it is still another major superpower.

But coming back, I see ASEAN as a major, major player and I think it is going to get even more so in the future. When you look around, I think Thailand is by far the strongest member of ASEAN and it's going to play a pivotal role in the development of this region. We see many people coming in to build factories here. And this could again be because nobody colonised Thailand and the Thais are always adjusting to American or Chinese influence. So I am as optimistic today about Thailand as I was in the 1960s because the country continues to maintain strong global relationships. They're going to be able to repeat that going into the next generation. That said, I do not underestimate the growth potential of other ASEAN countries, especially the CLMV (Cambodia/Laos/Myanmar/Vietnam). They have large populations, strong demographics and huge foreign direct investment, particularly in factories. These countries are also witnessing emerging middle-class consumers with an appetite to spend and try new things, which is great for hotels and restaurants".

The Minor Group will continue to get into new fields, new geographies, and make new acquisitions. In 2018, it made its biggest investment yet through the acquisition of one of the most prominent hotel chains in Europe, NH Hotel Group, for 2.3 billion euros, tripling the size of the hotel business. NH, based in Spain, is much larger than Minor, so the integration will be exciting though very challenging. Says Heinecke, "These next couple of years are going to be transformational times for us, as we become a global player competing on the world stage. And so, as much as I would like to be an investor today, I can't get out of the driver's seat, wanting to be a part of the action, not leaving it to someone else or being dependent on someone else to create the success. The years go by so quickly. You blink your eyes and suddenly find that you've been in business for 50 years.

When asked, "You've survived 50 years of challenges. Any regrets?" Heinecke sits back upright, "No, none whatsoever. I think there have certainly been times that I may have thought that I picked the wrong road, but in the end, no, I think all roads have been learning opportunities".

Endnote

1. William Heinecke, "The Entrepreneur: 25 Golden Rules for the Global Business Manager", Wiley, 30 January 2012.

ABOUT THE AUTHORS

Dr Philip Zerrillo is Professor of Marketing (Practice) at Singapore Management University, Singapore.

Dr Havovi Joshi is Director, Centre for Management Practice at Singapore Management University, Singapore.

Pannapachr Itthiopassagul is Assistant Professor of Marketing at Thammasat Business School, Bangkok, Thailand.